DR. ATKINS' *NEW* DIET COOKBOOK

DR. ATKINS' *NEW* DIET COOKBOOK

By Robert C. Atkins, M.D., and Fran Gare, M.S.

M. Evans and Company, Inc.
New York

We would like to especially acknowledge Nancy Mahoney, M.S., R.D., for her nutritional research on the recipes.

Copyright © 1994 by Robert C. Atkins, M.D.

M. Evans and Company, Inc.
216 East 49th Street
New York, New York 10017

Library of Congress Cataloging-in-Publication Data

Atkins, Robert C.
    [New Diet Cookbook]
    Dr. Atkins' new diet cookbook / Robert C. Atkins ; with recipes
and meal plans by Fran Gare
        p. cm.
    Includes index.
    ISBN 0-87131-755-9: $21.95
    1. Reducing diets. I. Mandell, Fran Gare. II. Title.
RM222.2.A842 1994
613.2'5—dc20   94-1273
                                                                  CIP

Design by Bernard Schleifer and Charles A. de Kay
Typeset by AeroType, Inc.
Manufactured in the United States of America
9 8 7 6 5 4 3 2 1

The advice offered in this book, although based on the author's experience with many thousands of patients, is not intended to be a substitute for the advice and counsel of your personal physician. Pregnant women and people with severe kidney disease are strongly advised not to follow this diet.

Contents

DR. ATKINS' *NEW* DIET COOKBOOK

1 | *Introduction*

You have all seen diet cookbooks, but for the past 20 years I suspect you haven't seen one like this. This isn't a copycat cookbook. It doesn't attempt to refurbish and bring to life the tired and repetitious diet styles of the recent past. In fact, if you start leafing through the recipes, you'll be in for the shock of your life. *Where's the diet?* you'll say. What happened to the austerity? No austerity, no diet, right? *Wrong!*

What sort of diet is this, then? Just glance at the wonderful, mouth-watering recipes Fran Gare has prepared for this book. Yes, they appear nondietetic because they're *not* fat-restricted. You quickly notice that oil, butter, and mayonnaise appear in them. *Why, Dr. Atkins, this is not the food of weight loss!* You tremble. Don't! This *is* the food of weight loss, and you can become slim eating it. (And, better yet, healthy.) But, I have to tell you that if you're relying on fat restriction to get you slim, this cookbook is certainly not for you.

On the other hand, if, like so many of the people I meet, you've been trying fat restriction and getting nowhere, I'll hazard a guess that this cookbook and the diet principles that go with it are exactly what you need.

You need a new start; new principles; a diet that works.

The success I promise is not done by magic. Low-carbohydrate dieting is the answer, and that means the application of well-attested facts about overweight that you've probably never heard about. Quite simply, since the late 1970s a simplistic theory of weight loss that focuses obsessively on dietary fat and by implication teaches the old, stale doctrine that gaining or losing weight is just a matter of calorie consumption has ruled the roost.

To know how simplistic it is to look at overweight that way, you only have to consider the different people you know, their different body types, and their different levels of appetite. Right away you'll see that there's no necessary connection between how much you eat and how heavy you are or between eating a lot of fat and being fat. You've surely noticed that folks who eat bacon and eggs for breakfast aren't consistently overweight. Nor folks who eat steaks or butter. Yet the restriction of fat has become the basis of a whole new weight-loss industry. Weight Watchers and its many imitators wage the battle of the bulge. Low-fat tips crowd the pages of women's magazines, and dire warnings resound from medical authorities on high.

And, as a result, we as a nation are without question and by all statistical measures eating less fat. The American public must be getting slimmer. Is it? That's a question I can easily answer. NHANES, the major government survey that tracks the weight patterns of the nation, found just last year that from 1980 to 1990, the percentage of overweight American adults went up from 26 percent of the population to 34 percent—a truly massive and astonishing 30 percent jump. If pudge-proneness is a virus, then tens of millions of us caught it even as we struggled to obey our antifat mentors.

Food for thought here. I know I haven't shocked you enough, so let me talk about eating. After all, this is a book that promises to be a source of the richest and most diverse dining pleasure. Disguise it though they may, most diet cookbook authors want to teach you how you can like carrot sticks and granola, skim milk and skinless chicken, celery stalks and butterless toast. They set a hard task for themselves. In their attempt to deploy a few delicious salads (though no more delicious than the ones our own Fran Gare will reveal to you), they are fundamentally working from poverty. Good cuisine has always rooted itself firmly in luxurious fat. That's why I feel confident you're going to relate to a diet and a cookbook that allows you New England Clam Chowder and Spicy Spareribs, Steak Au Poivre, Pâté and Roast Chicken, Duck in Red Wine, and desserts like Cheesecake and Chunky Chocolate Ice Cream.

I can see your mouth has fallen open, partly from appetite and partly from disbelief. *Dr. Atkins,* you're saying, *I heard you mention the merits of low carbohydrate dieting and I was perfectly willing to suspend my disbelief, but this is beyond the beyond. I've been reading magazine articles for the past dozen years trying to wean me from these delights. You're not serious!*

COULDN'T BE MORE SERIOUS, MY FRIEND

So, what gives? I'll tell you frankly out of my experience in advising overweight patients for a quarter of a century. In spite of all the hoopla and hysteria of the preceding years, most overweight men and women are *not* particularly sensitive to dietary fat.

What makes them fat and keeps them fat is a disorder of their *carbohydrate* metabolism. The foods they can't handle are *carbohydrate* foods. Trying to lose weight by fat restriction is torture for them because it doesn't address the *carbohydrate* basis of their problem.

Many of our major health problems and most of our weight problems are indeed nutritional, but they spring from eating the refined, processed, and devitalized food of the modern world, not from eating too many steaks or chicken breasts. I'd like to assure you that the health-problem foods that are really waiting to ambush you are sugar and sweeteners, hydrogenated oils and white flour, margarine and soda pop.

Do you realize that if you're overweight, there's a better than 90 percent chance that you have a problem with blood sugar and insulin levels? There's a very good chance that you are or will become diabetic. You're putting yourself at risk for heart disease. You probably suffer from fatigue and irritability that's totally curable if you eat a low-carbohydrate diet. And there's sound scientific evidence for what I'm telling you now that is largely being ignored.

I'd like to see you on the Atkins diet not just because it will slim you down remarkably, not just because it's delightful to imagine eating the delicious recipes Fran has prepared for you, but because you deserve to be a healthy person. The Atkins diet is a diet that reverses hypertension, controls diabetes, ends fatigue, corrects many eating and digestive disorders, and greatly reduces allergies.

Low-carbohydrate diets have often gotten a bum rap in the press and for that reason I hope that before you go on the Atkins diet you'll begin by having blood tests and measuring your blood pressure. After you've been on the diet for a few weeks, have these numbers checked again. Then, if your family or friends criticize you for doing something so unorthodox as ignoring the low-fat dogmas prevalent now, you'll be able to point to the irrefutable, numerical improvements in such health indicators as cholesterol and triglyceride levels and blood pressure. There's nothing like showing people that you're getting healthy even while they're watching you get slim.

INSULIN, OVERWEIGHT, AND YOU

If—as is most likely—you're among the overweight to whom my description of carbohydrate sensitivity applies, then your weight problem is caused by a problem with insulin, the hormone produced in the pancreas that we cannot live without. This is a scientific fact never mentioned in the weight-loss manuals of the antifat brigades.

Yet obesity is almost always found together with an excessive release of insulin after eating, the medical term for which is hyperinsulinism. When you eat, your body produces blood sugar (glucose). If you eat carbohydrate food, especially the refined carbohydrates I mentioned above, the glucose level goes up rapidly. Insulin is released to lower it. The insulin enables some of that glucose to be used for energy and stores the rest as . . . fat.

In fact, one wise scientist referred to insulin as "the fat-producing hormone."

Now if you want to lose weight, I've just told you the secret. Simply restrict the foods that stimulate excessive insulin release. Carbohydrates provide that kind of stimulation. Fats and proteins don't.

You simply need to severely restrict your consumption of carbohydrates (down to one or two small salads a day to start with), and you're on a weight-loss plan that has an unparalleled record of success.

And success doesn't stop when the pounds are off. I know you don't just want to lose weight, you want to keep it off.

Weight regain is the demon that bedevils dieters. They put time and effort and high hopes into adhering to a diet, and they lose 20 or 30, or perhaps 60 or 70 pounds, and then, presto, six months or eight months or a year after the diet is done they're back up where they were before. It's almost worse than never having lost.

No need for that on this diet plan. The Atkins maintenance diet is a natural transition from the initial weight-loss diet, and on it the vast majority of my dieters maintain their slimness. The lifetime diet you can move into once you're at your ideal weight is a healthy omnivorous diet that includes, meat, fish, fowl, vegetables, nuts, seeds, grains, and fruits and starches in moderation.

THIS IS WHAT YOU CAN EXPECT

Let me mention just a few of the things—besides good food—that you can expect to experience on the Atkins diet. Those of you who want to do the diet would be well advised to obtain *Dr. Atkins' New Diet Revolution* and learn step-by-step the essentials of successful low-carbohydrate dieting. I know many of you already have and now you're turning to this cookbook to make your diet experience more enjoyable. For those of you who are newcomers to the Atkins diet, this chapter aims to make it possible for you to begin the diet and carry it through with success. The final pages of this chapter give you the essential rules of such dieting, and the next chapter will explain the four stages of the Atkins lifetime-diet plan.

By following the simple rules, you'll find yourself on a weight-loss program that has the following surprising characteristics. Study them carefully for very few diets can claim even one of them.

This is a diet that:

- Sets no limit on the amount of food you can eat.
- Completely excludes hunger from the dieting experience.
- Includes rich and luxurious foods that you've never associated with dieting before.
- Reduces your appetite by a perfectly natural function of the body.
- Gives you a metabolic edge so significant that the whole concept of watching calories will become absurd to you.
- Produces steady weight loss, even if you have experienced dramatic failures on other diets.
- Is so perfectly adapted to use as as lifetime diet that, unlike most diets, the lost weight won't come back.
- Consistently produces improvements in most of the health problems that accompany overweight.

I'm sure you wonder how all this is possible. Why does the diet work? How will my appetite be reduced? What's all this talk of a metabolic edge? Those were all the questions I hoped you'd ask. Listen.

KETOSIS/LIPOLYSIS
On the Atkins diet, you'll lose weight without hunger. To most dieters that's the miraculous part. No more counting calories, skimping on portions, rising from the table with an ache of appetite still present and unaccounted for. I not only tell my dieters, *Well, if you're hungry, eat!* but I take pleasure in the fact that low-carbohydrate dieting suppresses appetite. Most of you will find that the change in your appetite level is one of the most astonishing experiences of your dieting life.

You see, your body was designed to suppress hunger during periods of food deprivation. If any of you have fasted or watched other people fast, you'll have noticed that after the first two days hunger disappears. Carbohydrate restriction produces the same phenomenon.

What does the body of a faster or a low-carbohydrate dieter do to provide energy? It burns off its own stored fat. In the case of a fast you'll also burn off muscle tissue, which is not advisable and can even be dangerous. On a low-carbohydrate diet, you burn off *nothing but fat.*

In the metabolic pecking order, the first fuel that the body uses for energy—glucose—is derived from carbohydrate food. But when you drastically restrict carbohydrate intake, very little glucose is produced in your bloodstream after you've eaten. Your crafty metabolism appraises the alternatives and for two days after the diet begins it turns to stored carbohydrate (called glycogen) to power its operations. Once that is gone, your body moves down the pecking order. It turns to its own fat for fuel. Presto! you've begun to lose weight.

You enter a state called ketosis because among the by-products of fat burning are compounds called ketone bodies. They're your new-found source of energy. Be assured, your body is just as happy using them as it was using glucose. Another name for the whole process is lipolysis, which means "the dissolving of fat."

As you go into ketosis/lipolysis, the appetite suppression I just mentioned occurs. Because this usually results in a decrease in your intake of calories, your rate of weight loss is accelerated. But if you continue to eat as many calories as you did before the diet started, you will generally lose weight anyway only at a slower pace.

YOUR METABOLIC ADVANTAGE

This "extra" weight loss is the result of a very exciting side benefit of low-carbohydrate dieting called a metabolic advantage. Very simply— and this has been repeatedly demonstrated in scientific studies—*a person who's eating a strict low-carbohydrate diet loses more weight at whatever his or her level of caloric intake is than he or she would be losing if eating the same number of calories on any other type of diet.* Startling, but at least ten studies conducted in the '60s, '70s, and '80s demonstrated that effect. A low-carbohydrate diet is a calorically wasteful diet. More calories are burned off by your metabolism than on any other diet.

I'm sure I don't need to tell you what an advantage this is. You don't need to concentrate on restricting calories; all you need to do is keep your intake of carbohydrate at such a level that you're in ketosis and enjoying the metabolic advantage nature has provided for you. From that there automatically follows appetite suppression and accelerated rate of weight loss per unit of caloric intake.

Let me emphasize one simple fact: Your body *wants* you to use up your fat stores. It elaborates all sorts of messenger chemicals to facilitate the burning of your stored fat—they're called fat mobilizers. The fat mobilizers redirect your metabolic processes so that you comfortably switch from your normal sugar-burning pathway to the alternative pathway where fat is your body's—and your brain's—primary fuel.

Ketosis/lipolysis is the happiest condition a dieter can be in. Not only does it work, but it requires no willpower, no hunger, and no suffering of any kind. After two or three days of adjustment to the diet, most of you will feel better and more energetic than you've felt in years.

Being on the Atkins diet is a great convincer, but you have to bring some degree of resolution and commitment to your nutritional changeover. A halfhearted low-carbohydrate diet may make you feel physically better, but it probably won't produce much weight loss. Smooth, consistent weight loss is a consequence of so severely restricting carbohydrate intake that you do go into ketosis and begin to burn your own fat for fuel.

To do this you must initially cut down your carbohydrates to one or two small salads or a salad and a helping of vegetables per day. Bread, pasta, sugar, and starchy foods in general will not be allowed while you're in the weight-loss phase of your diet plan. Once you've reached your ideal weight you'll be able to cautiously increase your intake of carbohydrate foods.

OTHER ESSENTIALS OF THE ATKINS DIET

Knowing whether you're in ketosis/lipolysis or not is obviously crucial to your success. Some people play it by ear (or ounce). If they're losing weight they know they're following the game plan. I think it's more effective to get Bioketone testing strips, which you can put in your urine once a day (preferably in the evening). If the strips turn purple, you know you're in ketosis.

Another crucial aspect of dietary success is nutritional supplementation. In the strict early phase of the diet, which I call the Induction phase, you'll need vitamins and minerals to keep you at a healthy level for all nutrients. Even when you're at the advanced and more liberalized levels of the diet I strongly advise supplementation because it's good for you. See "Nutritional Supplementation" in the appendices for a description of what your basic multivitamin formula should include.

BE PREPARED

My other advice for the beginning Atkins dieter is in the area of preparation. Prepare your relatives and prepare your kitchen. Qualitatively speaking, this is a strict diet. There's no room for cheating. I can already hear your spouse saying, "Just this one little piece of cake won't hurt you." It will. You can't do the diet that way.

So start by telling the folks you live with just what you intend to do. Tell them that you take your diet seriously, and you'd appreciate their doing the same. If they question the wisdom of a high-protein diet that isn't interested in fat restriction, tell them to watch and wait. When they see how terrific you feel and how good you look, their temptation to criticize will start to fade away. Be diplomatic and gentle but firm. Eating is a very emotional habit, and changes in the way you eat affect everyone around you. Nonetheless, this is your diet, not your relatives'.

As for your kitchen, if you live alone it will be easy. Invite some friends over to finish off the ice cream, and give all your forbidden foods away to friends and neighbors. If there are others in the house, and they're not going to be on this diet, then simply see that there are separate portions of such forbidden foods as bread, potatoes, and sugar-laden deserts for them. The main course, the salads, and the vegetables will be suitable for everyone.

Now, before you turn to the wonderful part of this book (the food!), look at the next chapter and make sure you know how you'll do the series of diets that together comprise the Atkins diet. This is going to be your gateway to a lifetime of eating pleasure and dieting success.

2 | *Four Diets in One*

This chapter is designed for those of you who haven't read *Dr. Atkins' New Diet Revolution*. It will give, I hope, a simple and effective description of the Atkins diet in its four stages.

These are:

1. The Induction Diet
2. The Ongoing Weight-Loss Diet
3. The Premaintenance Diet
4. The Maintenance Diet

These four stages are an effective way of breaking up and explaining what—for you—will be one continuous lifetime diet. The Induction diet gets you into weight loss with a bang; the Ongoing Weight-Loss diet carries you through the weeks or months of weight loss needed to get you close to your ideal weight; the Premaintenance diet takes you the final few steps and eases your transition to what is perhaps the most important diet of all; and that is the Maintenance diet—your lifetime ticket to health and slimness. Let's take them in order.

GETTING STARTED

The Induction diet—your start-up diet—is very strict in its limitation of carbohydrates. *Because of its rigor, this phase of the diet is not appropriate for pregnant women and people with severe kidney disease.* You'll only be eating 15 to 20 grams of carbohydrates on it, which might be two medium salads and a helping of vegetables. The purpose of this strictness is to ensure that your body does indeed go into ketosis/lipolysis, does begin releasing fat-mobilizing hormones that will suppress your appetite, and does, after the first two or three days, begin to consume your own fat. This is what you're working toward initially, and your success is pretty well assured.

Once you're in ketosis, your body has made a transition from burning carbohydrate (glucose) for fuel to employing its alternative metabolic pathway that was evolved millions of years ago to enable you to survive periods of famine. You now break down fat, and the by-products of this fat breakdown—ketone bodies—are consumed for energy.

This is the basic Atkins diet, so let me explain it in full. The other three diets are careful, gradual liberalizations of the Induction diet, and they'll be easy to explain once you're grounded in the Induction diet.

THE RULES OF THE INDUCTION DIET

1. *Your diet must contain no more than 20 grams of carbohydrate a day.* For most people, induction of ketosis/lipolysis can be achieved on this intake. This allows for approximately 3 cups of salad vegetables (loosely packed) or 2 cups of salad plus ⅔ cup of cooked vegetables in the below 10 percent carbohydrate category.
2. You are no longer on a quantitative diet. Therefore you should adjust the quantities to your appetite. When hungry, eat the amount that makes you feel satisfied but not stuffed. When not hungry, eat nothing or just a small protein snack to accompany your vitamins.
3. You are, however, on a qualitative diet. This means that if the food is not on your diet, you are to have absolutely none of it. Your "just this one taste won't hurt" rationalization is the kiss of death on this diet. Addicts will find this rule builds character in a hurry.
4. Your diet will consist of pure proteins (not many of those in nature, however), pure fats (this means butter, olive oil, and mayonnaise are permitted), and combinations of protein and fat (this is the mainstay of your diet). Foods that are protein-and-carbohydrate or fat-and-carbohydrate are *not* on this diet, because carbohydrate is not on this diet.
5. Using a carbohydrate gram counter, one could find other combinations totaling less than 20 grams of carbohydrate. One would be using foods like nuts, seeds, olives, avocados,

cheeses, cream and sour cream, lemon and lime juices, and low-carbohydrate diet foods. Don't assume these foods are low, unless you absolutely know the carbohydrate content of the portion you are eating. In the Carbohydrate Gram Counter on page 230, I will include the carbohydrate content in grams of the foods you may include on this 14-day *Induction* diet as well as on more liberal levels of the diet that you will be doing as your lifetime diet plan.

FREE FOODS:

MEAT	FISH	FOWL
Beef	Tuna	Chicken
Pork	Salmon	Turkey
Lamb	Sole	Duck
Bacon	Trout	Goose
Veal	Flounder	Cornish Hen
Ham	Sardines	Quail
Venison	Herring	Pheasant
in fact, all meat	*in fact, all fish*	*in fact, all fowl*

SHELLFISH	EGGS	CHEESE
Oysters	Scrambled	Aged and fresh
Mussels	Fried	Cow and goat
Clams	Poached	Cream cheese
Squid	Soft Boiled	Cottage cheese
Shrimp	Hard Boiled	Swiss
Lobster	Deviled	Cheddar
Crabmeat	Omelets	Mozzarella
in fact, all shellfish	*in fact, all eggs*	*in fact, almost* all cheeses*

Exceptions: 1) luncheon meats with nitrites or sugar added
2) products that are not exclusively meat, fish, or fowl, such as imitation fish

---

*All cheeses have some carbohydrate content, and quantities are governed by that. (See Carbohydrate Gram Counter.) No diet cheese, cheese spreads, or whey cheeses. Those with a known yeast infection, dairy allergy, or cheese intolerance must avoid cheese. Imitation cheese products are not allowed, except for Tofu (soy cheese)—but check carbohydrate content.

OTHER INDUCTION DIET FOODS:

Vegetables of 10 Percent Carbohydrate or Less

SALAD VEGETABLES:

Alfalfa Sprouts	Endive	Parsley
Arugula	Escarole	Peppers
Bok Choy	Fennel	Posse Pied
Boston Lettuce	Jicama	Radicchio
Celery	Mache	Radishes
Chicory	Morels	Romaine
Chives	Mushrooms	Sorrel
Cucumber	Olives	

SALAD HERBS:

Basil	Dill	Rosemary
Cilantro	Oregano	Thyme

For salad dressing use the desired oil plus vinegar or lemon juice and spices. Grated cheese, chopped eggs, bacon, or fried pork rinds may be added.

VEGETABLES IN ADDITION TO SALAD VEGETABLES:

Artichoke Hearts	Christophene	Sauerkraut
Asparagus	Collard Greens	Scallions
Avocado	Dandelion Greens	Snow Pea Pods
Bamboo Shoots	Eggplant	Spaghetti Squash
Bean Sprouts	Hearts of Palm	Spinach
Beet Greens	Kale	String or Wax Beans
Broccoli	Kohlrabi	Summer Squash
Brussels Sprouts	Leeks	Tomato
Cabbage	Okra	Turnips
Cauliflower	Onion	Water Chestnuts
Celery Root (celeriac)	Pumpkin	Zucchini Squash
Chard	Rhubarb	

SALAD GARNISHES:

Anchovies	Minced Hard-Boiled Egg Yolk
Crumbled Crisp Bacon	Minced Sautéed Mushrooms
Grated Cheese	Sour Cream

SPICES:

All spices to taste, but make sure sugar is not in the seasoning.

BEVERAGES:

Water
Mineral Water
Essence Flavored Seltzer
  (must say "No Calories")
Decaffinated coffee or tea
Diet Soda (read label)
Iced tea with artificial sweetener
Cream (heavy or light);
  note carbohydrate content
Natural and artificial orange
  soda products have some
  carbohydrate—they may be
  one of your options for a few
  grams

Spring Water
Club Soda
Herb Tea
  (no barley, dates, figs, sugar)
Caffeine is not allowed
Carbohydrate free, artificially
  sweetened powder for making
  fruit-flavored drinks
Clear broth/bouillon (not all
  brands)
Grain Beverages (i.e., imitation
  coffee substitutes) are *not*
  allowed

FATS AND OILS:

Many fats, especially certain oils, are essential to good nutrition. Include a source a GLA (gamma-linolnic acid) and omega-3 oils (EPA, salmon oil, linseed oil). Olive oil (monounsaturated) is valuable. All vegetable oils are allowed. The best are canola, walnut, soybean, sesame, sunflower, and safflower oils, especially if they are labeled "cold pressed." Butter is allowed; margarine is not. Margarine should be avoided not because of its carbohydrate content but because it is a potential health hazard. Mayonnaise is permitted unless you are on a yeast restriction. The fat that is part of the meat or fowl you eat is permitted.

Avoid the seeming paradox provide by today's "diet foods." Understand why cream is allowed but not skim milk, why sour cream can be used but not yogurt, why low-fat chicken breading is not allowed even though chicken may be pan-fried. The answer common to all of these seeming inconsistencies lies in the higher carbohydrate content of the low-fat dieter's foods.

ARTIFICIAL SWEETENERS:

Dieters must determine which artificial sweeteners agree with them, but the following are allowed: saccharine, aspartame, acesulfame-K.

Sweeteners such as sorbitol, mannitol, and other hexitols are not allowed, nor are any natural sweeteners ending in the letters -ose, such as maltose, fructose, and so on.

COMMON MISTAKES TO AVOID:

1. Note that the 14-day diet contains no fruit, bread, grains, starchy vegetables, dairy products other than cheese, cream, or butter.
2. Avoid diet products unless they specifically state "No carbohydrates." Most dietetic foods are for fat-restricted, not carbohydrate-restricted, diets.
3. The word sugarless is not sufficient. The product must state the carbohydrate content, and that's what you go by.
4. Many products you do not normally think of as foods such as chewing gum, cough syrups, and cough drops are filled with sugar and other caloric sweeteners and must be avoided.

THE ONGOING WEIGHT-LOSS DIET

You won't need to do the Induction diet for more than a couple of weeks. By that time, I feel confident that you'll not only be losing weight but feeling healthier than you have in years. Most people feel energized by a low-carbohydrate diet. On the weight-loss front, most of you will have seen five to ten pounds disappear, and that means you can now liberalize your intake of carbohydrate slightly. You've begun the Ongoing Weight-Loss diet, which will carry you pleasantly along for as many weeks or months as it takes to get you very close to your ideal weight.

This minor liberalization of carbohydrate is, of course, not an invitation to go back to eating the way you did before. What, in fact, you'll be doing is increasing the daily amount of carbohydrate by 5 grams at a time. You'll do this very gradually because you don't want to fall out of ketosis/lipolysis. I suggest that each week you increase your daily carbohydrate consumption by 5 grams. Typical 5-gram increments are 10 Brazil nuts or 20 macadamias, or half of an avocado or half a tomato, or 3 ounces of plain, unflavored yogurt, or ⅔ of a cup of string beans or broccoli or 2½ wafers of GG Bran Crispbread.

Those of you who have been chafing at the absolute restriction of alcohol on the Induction diet might now add 4 ounces of dry wine or 6 ounces of a light beer, or 1 ounce of whiskey or gin daily.

Yeast Infections

I have to tell you a little bit about yeast infections because—if you have them—they could derail your diet and blight your predestined dieting success.

In my experience, more than a quarter of the patients I see have an overgrowth of one particular yeast, which is known as *Candida albicans.* *Candida* is a normal part of your body, one of four hundred species of bacteria resident in the human intestinal tract. In healthy competition with your other intestinal flora, *Candida* serves you well performing yeasty bacterial mission in your gut. But when some disturbance upsets the bacterial equilibrium in your body, a yeast infection can ensue. *Candida* overgrows, suppresses less aggressive bacteria, and causes a multitude of symptoms.

A short list of the problems a yeast infection can cause include lethargy; fatigue; depression; inability to concentrate; headaches; gastrointestinal disorders, including constipation, abdominal pain, gas, diarrhea, and bloating; respiratory ailments, and disorders of the urinary tract and reproductive organs. The most specific symptom is bloating—gas in the lower abdomen.

Let me repeat: A *Candida albicans* yeast infection will also make it very difficult to lose weight.

The four most common contributing causes to a yeast infection are:

1. A diet high in sugar and refined carbohydrates.
2. Antibiotics (more than 20 weeks in a lifetime would make *Candida* overgrowth a probability).
3. The mercury in silver dental fillings.
4. Birth control pills, prednisone, and other steroids.

This is an embarrassing list for medicine since the last three provokers of yeast overgrowth are all related to medical care. Perhaps that explains why *Candida* hasn't received nearly the attention it deserves.

If you think you have a yeast infection, you may need to see a physician who's experienced in treating them. In *Dr. Atkins' New Diet Revolution* I devote a chapter to *Candida* and its treatments. For now, let me simply say that whatever therapies your doctor proposes, he will certainly also tell you that you need to make alterations in the way you eat. Fermented and yeast-containing foods are inappropriate for a person who's suffering from yeast overgrowth. Please turn to the section on the yeast-free diet for further information on this dietary problem.

Of course, as you increase your carbohydrate consumption, you will see a gradual decrease in your rate of weight loss. That's fine. The purpose of this diet is not to lose weight in a hurry, but to get it off and *keep it off.* By slowing down your rate of loss, you go gradually toward your ultimate diet.

THE PREMAINTENANCE DIET

The Premaintenance diet is a further extension of the diet liberalization that you went toward on the Ongoing Weight-Loss diet. When you're getting fairly close to your ultimate goal weight, it's very important that you lose weight slowly. Many of you are such determined dieters that this will be psychologically burdensome. You've got that final five or six pounds to go, you know you can do it in two weeks, why postpone success? Sorry, folks, that's not the best way to proceed. I think you should carve off those final pounds over the course of two or three months. Here's why.

The biggest problem with weight control is not the losing but the maintenance. How many celebrity dieters have you heard of who lost their weight in a crash program and then gained it back faster than they lost it? What you should do is just the opposite. Lose those final pounds with excruciating slowness so that by the time you say, "I'm there!" you'll be virtually eating your lifetime diet.

As for doing Premaintenance, it's simple. Either add another 10 grams of carbohydrate a day to what you've been eating on Ongoing Weight-Loss, or give yourself a 20-gram carbohydrate treat two or three times a week. You can even touch some forbidden starches. A bagel, a baked potato, some French toast, a slice of pizza, a side dish of lasagna. Or else add some of your favorite fruits—apples, oranges, grapefruits, peaches, bananas. As long as you don't start gaining weight but continue to lose at an almost imperceptible rate, you're doing fine.

GOING ON YOUR LIFETIME MAINTENANCE DIET

Now that you've arrived, offer yourself some well-deserved self-congratulation, and prepare for a slim lifetime.

As you already know, there's no shortage of delicious food for you to eat. The one scientific fact of importance that you must be aware of, however, is that once you've totally stopped your weight loss, your appetite will increase toward its normal level. For this reason, your lifetime maintenance diet will still be fairly restrictive of carbohydrate foods.

You'll need to find your own level, and that level will be what I call your Critical Carbohydrate Level for Maintenance. This is the level *above* which you *gain* weight. At this level, you will have enough carbohydrate restriction to keep *some* curbing of your appetite, and, for most of you, this will range between 40 and 90 grams of carbohydrate a day. Still considerably less than the average American consumption of 300 grams a day!

Here are my final suggestions for you happy dieters who have now reached your ideal weight.

1. Be food aware—meat, fish, fowl, nuts, seeds, vegetables, and occasional fruits and starches are the foods nature designed you to eat. Avoid processed foods. Eat fresh and natural to the best of your ability.
2. Avoid sugar and corn syrup and white flour and cornstarch like the plague. For most people these are the foods of overweight and ill health.
3. Individualize your diet. Try new foods. Create the diet that's right for you.
4. Consider the program of vitamin and mineral supplementation that's explained in Appendix 1 and that you've been using while you were on the weight-loss portion of the diet.
5. Use caffeine and alcohol in moderation.
6. If you regain more than five pounds of weight go right back to the Induction diet. Within two weeks you should find yourself back at your ideal weight.
7. Please do exercise. Though there isn't time to talk about it here, it's wonderful for health and very helpful in maintaining slimness.

Now for a final word about eating. . . .

ARE YOU READY TO BE HAPPY?

I can't guarantee that I'll make you wealthy and wise, but I have every intention of making you happy in your body. That doesn't just mean slim, it also means healthy and thrilled by the food you eat. It's simply essential that your foods thrill you. If they don't, how can I fulfill my promise that for you the Atkins diet will be a lifetime diet?

I want your new meals to provide you with every bit as much emotional satisfaction and eating happiness as your normal pre-Atkins way of eating did. Hopefully more. If we succeed at this, then there will be no reason for you to return to your old way of eating—the way that didn't work.

If you follow the suggestions that that ever-so-talented food wizard, Fran Gare, has prepared for you in this book, you probably end up much better at cooking than you were before. This is no small advantage. Add to that the fact that on the Atkins maintenance diet, you will be eating sufficient fat to produce satiety and avoid disruptive blood sugar patterns, and I think you're an odds-on favorite to succeed.

Let me give you a dieting tip. One of the advantages of fat in your diet is that it buffers your changing blood sugar levels, it prevents swift, disturbing changes, and it thereby suppresses the craving for sweets. The successful effort to lower the amount of fat in the American diet over the past two decades has been bought at a crippling price. During this same period the American consumption of sugar has increased by 20 pounds yearly. That's not only a catastrophe for dieters but a catastrophe for health.

You may have heard of the French paradox. The French consume more fat than Americans (including four times as much butter and twice as much cheese), but they have less than half our heart attack rate. How can this be? It demands an answer, and the theorists of low fat have done a spectacularly ineffectual job of providing one. But the true answer is evident. We eat three times as much sugar as the French, and the research linking sugar to excess insulin production to heart disease is strong and growing stronger.

So don't be afraid of fat. Not only can you use it for weight loss, you can eat it in good health. The Atkins diet is not a high-fat diet since many of the junk food sources of fat are not permitted on it, but it is a diet that's unafraid of fat. The lifetime maintenance diet that will keep you slim is natural for human beings and well suited to the improvement of your health.

As you succeed on the Atkins diet and eat the scrumptious recipes Fran Gare has prepared for you, there will be one final question you'll have to ask yourself: Am I happier eating this way than I was before? Personally, I think nothing compares with smelling a delectable main course sizzling in the frying pan and experiencing appetite combined with the sure and certain knowledge that appetite is shortly to be gratified.

On many other diets people are asked, "Are you satisfied with the food," and often they'll reply, "Oh, yes, I'm satisfied." All too often, these responses fail the acid test of dieting: The hopeful dieters who made them end up gaining their weight back and resuming their former eating patterns.

But so seldom does that happen with the diet you're committed to trying now. So very seldom. And, of course, that's because dieters *are* happier eating the Atkins way. Most of them feel better than they've felt in years, all of them look better, and, far from feeling deprived, they're luxuriating in a whole new world of delicious foods.

And now that I've said the magic words, *delicious foods,* please proceed to the rest of the book. I leave you in the capable hands of Fran Gare.

3 | *Meal Plans*

The Induction Diet

SEVEN-DAY MENUS
DAY 1

Breakfast

> 2–3 Eggs, *Poached, *Hard or Soft Boiled
> 4 slices no-nitrate bacon
> 1 ounce Cheddar cheese
> Tea or decaffinated coffee with 1 tablespoon cream and sugar
> substitute

Lunch

> *Chicken Salad Ham Rolls
> *Orange Cooler

Dinner

> *Spicy Cocktail
> *Luscious Lamb
> Tossed green salad with *Vinaigrette Cream Dressing

Snack

> *Snappy Raspberries and Lemons

---

*Those dishes noted with an asterick are found in Chapter 4, Recipes.

DAY 2

Breakfast

*Scrambled or *Sunny-Side-Up and Over Easy eggs
2 slices smoked ham wrapped around a celery stick stuffed with 1 tablespoon of cream cheese
Tea or decaffinated coffee with 1 tablespoon cream and sugar substitute

Lunch

*¡Ole! Burger
½ cucumber, sliced, sprinkled with cayenne pepper
*Shape-Up-Shake

Dinner

*Salami and Parmesan
*Fabulous Flounder
Tossed green salad with *Lime Dill Dressing
Tea or decaffinated coffee with 1 tablespoon cream and sugar substitute

Snack

*Hot Mint Chocolate Nog

DAY 3

Breakfast

*Cheese-Baked Eggs
2 sausage patties
Tea or decaffinated coffee with 1 tablespoon cream and sugar substitute

Lunch

*Chicken Croquettes on a bed of lettuce
*Orange Cooler

Dinner

*Sour Cream Clam Dip with Fried Pork Rinds
*Fennel Red Snapper
Tossed green salad with *Dressing of the House
Tea or decaffinated coffee with 1 tablespoon cream and sugar substitute

Snack

*Vanilla Ice Cream

DAY 4

Breakfast

*Mocha Drink
*Herb Omelet

Lunch

*Sardine snack on lettuce leaves
Sliced celery and olives
Tea or decaffinated coffee with 1 tablespoon cream and sugar substitute

Dinner

*Tomato Lemon Jell-O
*Lemon-Basted Roast Chicken
*Ricotta Sauce for Chicken

Tea or decaffinated coffee with 1 tablespoon cream and sugar substitute

Snack

*Sweet Lemonade with Lecithin

DAY 5

Breakfast

4 *Deviled-Salmon Egg halves
2 1-gram crisp breads (GG is an example)
*Spiced Iced Decaf Coffee

Lunch

*Fresh Tuna and Avocado Salad
*Spicy Cocktail

Dinner

*Japanese Egg Custard Soup
*Oriental Shrimp
*Raspberry Jell-O Cream
Tea or decaffinated coffee with 1 tablespoon cream and sugar substitute

Snack

*Sour Cream Clam Dip with Fried Pork Rinds

DAY 6

Breakfast

*Spicy Sausage Omelet
2 ounces cheese of your choice
Tea or decaffinated coffee with 1 tablespoon cream and sugar substitute

Lunch

*U.S. Hamburgers
Tossed green salad with *Our Favorite Roquefort Dressing
Diet soda or diet iced tea

Dinner

*Chicken Stock with *Dumplings
*Gourmet Game Hens
*Crispy White Radish
*Vanilla Ice Cream
Tea or decaffinated coffee with 1 tablespoon cream and sugar substitute

Snack

*The 'Pop' Pop

DAY 7

Breakfast

Steak and *Scrambled Eggs with 2 tablespoons *Cheese Sauce
Tea or decaffinated coffee with 1 tablespoon cream and sugar substitute

Lunch

*Creamy Ricotta Soup
Tuna in olive oil with lemon wedge
½ cucumber, sliced
2 tablespoons *Mustard Vinaigrette
Tea or decaffinated coffee with 1 tablespoon cream and sugar substitute

Dinner

5 *Swedish Meatballs
*Shrimp Parmesan
Tossed salad with *Tomato Dressing
*Mocha Drink

Snack

½ cup *Maple Walnut Ice Cream

The Ongoing Weight-Loss Diet

DAY 1

Breakfast

*Two-Cheese Omelet
3 strips no-nitrate bacon
1 slice *4 Grain and Seed Bread
Tea or decaffinated coffee with 1 tablespoon cream and sugar substitute

Lunch

*Eggplant Parmigiana
Tossed green salad with *Italian Dressing
*Orange Cooler

Dinner

*Caribbean Crabmeat
*Halibut Roll-Ups
*Broccoli in Cheese Sauce
Tea or decaffinated coffee with 1 tablespoon cream and sugar substitute

Snack

2 squares of *Chocolate Fudge
Diet soda

DAY 2

Breakfast

*Poached Eggs on ham with 2 tablespoons *Hollandaise Sauce
2 slices *4 Grain and Seed Bread
Tea or decaffinated coffee with 1 tablespoon of cream and sugar substitute

Lunch

*Chicken Salad
6 Fried Pork Rinds

Diet soda or diet iced tea

Dinner

*Enchiladas
Tossed green salad with *Dressing of the House
*Baked Cream
Tea or decaffinated coffee with 1 tablespoon of cream and sugar substitute

Snack

*Spiced Iced Coffee
2 *Peanut Butter Cookies

DAY 3

Breakfast

*Crabmeat and Mushroom Omelet
2 slices *Rye Bread with cream cheese
Tea or decaffinated coffee with 1 tablespoon of cream and sugar substitute

Lunch

*Dr. Atkins' Fromage Burger
½ tomato, sliced
¼ cucumber, sliced
Diet soda

Dinner

*New England Fish Chowder
*Broiled Tarragon Lobster Tails
*Porcini Mushrooms
*Raspberry Cream Jell-O
Tea or decaffinated coffee with 1 tablespoon of cream and sugar substitute

Snack

2 *Almond Ball Cookies

DAY 4

Breakfast

> *Rye Bread, smoked salmon and cream cheese
> 2 slices onion
> Tea or decaffinated coffee with 1 tablespoon cream and sugar substitute

Lunch

> *Ham and Artichoke Omelet
> Tossed green salad with *Basic French Dressing
> 1 slice *Cheese Cake
> Iced decaffinated coffee with cream

Dinner

> *Fran's Special Pâté
> Roast Beef with *Frozen Horseradish Cream
> Endive with *Caesar Parmesan Dressing
> Tea or decaffinated coffee with 1 tablespoon of cream and sugar substitute

Snack

> ½ cup *Decaf Coffee Ice Cream

DAY 5

Breakfast

> *Two-Cheese Omelet
> 4 slices crisp bacon
> 2 slices *4 Grain and Seed Bread

Lunch

> *Vegetable Stock with *Creamy Dumplings
> *Zucchini Stuffed with Cream Sauce
> Romaine lettuce with *Mustard Vinaigrette
> Diet soda

Dinner

> *Sardine Snack stuffed into celery sticks

*Fennel Red Snapper
*Chic Asparagus
*Tomato-Lemon Jell-O
Tea or decaffinated coffee with 1 tablespoon cream and sugar
substitute

Snack

2 *Brownie Squares

DAY 6

Breakfast

*Cappuccino
*Scrambled Eggs with ham and *Mustard Sauce
1 slice *Rye Bread with cream cheese
Tea or decaffinated coffee with 1 tablespoon cream and sugar
substitute

Lunch

*Houston's Ceviche
*Orange Cooler

Dinner

*Tricolor Salad with Three Cheeses
*Chicken à la Firenze
½ small tomato, sliced
Tea or decaffinated coffee with 1 tablespoon of cream and sugar
substitute

Snack

Diet Jell-O with 1 tablespoon of whipped cream

DAY 7

Breakfast

Smoked whitefish with scallion cream cheese on 2 slices *Rye Bread
*Scrambled Eggs
Tea or decaffinated coffee with 1 teaspoon of cream and sugar substitute

Lunch

*U.S. Hamburgers with 1 slice of onion and lettuce
*Chocolate Shake

Dinner

*Cream of Shiitake Mushroom Soup
*Chicken Croquettes served on spaghetti squash
Tossed green salad with *Dill Vinaigrette Dressing

Snack

*Butter Pecan Ice Cream
Diet soda

The Premaintenance Diet

DAY 1

Breakfast

> *Turkey Sausage
> Scrambled Eggs
> 2 slices *Zucchini Bread

Lunch

> *Crunchy Seafood Salad
> *Vanilla Ice Cream
> *Diet soda

Dinner

> ¼ Cantaloupe with lemon slice
> *Stuffed Steak
> *Ratatouille
> *Lemon-Lime Mousse
> Tea or decaffinated coffee with 1 tablespoon cream and sugar substitute

Snack

> 2 ounces (20) macadamia nuts or
> ½ cup *Coconut-Macadamia Ice Cream

DAY 2

Breakfast

> *Eggplant and Cheddar Omelet
> ¼ pound grilled ham
> 2 slices *Rye Bread

Lunch

> *Fresh Tuna and Avocado Salad
> 3 1-gram crisp breads (GG is an example)
> *Fresh Lemonade with Lecithin

Dinner

> *Manicotti
> *Green Bean Chokes
> *Tomato-Lemon Jell-O on lettuce leaves
> Tea or decaffinated coffee with 1 tablespoon cream and sugar substitute

Snack

> 2 ounces almonds

DAY 3

Breakfast

> French toast made with 4 slices *4 Grain and Seed Bread dipped into a beaten egg and fried in butter
> 4 slices of crisp no-nitrate bacon
> Tea or decaffinated coffee with 1 tablespoon cream and sugar substitute

Lunch

> *Hot Beef Salad
> *Orange Cooler

Dinner

> *Canneloni with Chicken
> 1 cup steamed broccoli
> Tossed salad with *Tomato Mayonnaise

*Italian Rum Cake
Tea or decaffinated coffee with 1 tablespoon cream and sugar
substitute

Snack

¼ cup fresh raspberries and 2 tablespoons whipped cream

DAY 4

Breakfast

Your favorite cut of steak, sliced
*Scrambled Eggs with *Hot Barbecue Sauce
Tea or decaffinated coffee with 1 tablespoon cream and sugar
substitute

Lunch

*Salad Niçoise With Fresh Tuna
2 slices *Rye Bread and butter
Diet soda
*Lemon Jell-O Cream

Dinner

*Enchiladas
Tossed green salad with *Creamy Celery Dressing
*The Most Delicious Cucumbers
Tea or decaffinated coffee with 1 tablespoon cream and sugar
substitute

Snack

½ cup *Decaf Coffee Ice Cream

DAY 5

Breakfast

> Smoked salmon, onions, and eggs scrambled
> 2 slices *Zucchini Bread with scallion cream cheese
> Tea or decaffinated coffee with 1 tablespoon cream and sugar
> substitute

Lunch

> *Eggplant Little Shoes
> Tossed green salad with *Italian Dressing
> Tea or decaffinated coffee with 1 tablespoon cream and sugar
> substitute

Dinner

> *Fish Stock with *Dumplings
> *Sun Luck Scallops
> *Chic Asparagus
> Tea or decaffinated coffee with 1 tablespoon cream and sugar
> substitute

Snack

> 3 *Almond Ball Cookies

DAY 6

Breakfast

> *Shrimp and Goat Cheese Omelet
> 2 slices *4 Grain and Seed Bread
> Tea or decaffinated coffee with 1 tablespoon cream and sugar
> substitute

Lunch

> *Poached Salmon Salad
> 3 1-gram crisp breads (GG is an example)
> Tea or decaffinated coffee with 1 tablespoon cream and sugar
> substitute

Dinner

  *Vichyssoise with Dill and Caraway
  *Gourmet Pork Chops
  *String Beans Almondine
  *Crispy White Radish
  Tea or decaffinated coffee with 1 tablespoon cream and sugar
  substitute

Snack

  ½ cup *Maple Walnut Ice Cream

DAY 7

Breakfast

  *Peaches and Cream Omelet
  *Hot Chocolate

Lunch

  ½ cantaloupe stuffed with *A Mold of Roquefort
  *Tuna Loaf
  Iced tea or iced coffee

Dinner

  *Roast Turkey With Almond Stuffing
  *Irene's Turnips
  *Baked Spinach
  ½ cup *Peach Melba Frozen Yogurt
  Tea or decaffinated coffee with 1 tablespoon cream and sugar
  substitute

Snack

  2 ounces pecans (about 20)

The Yeast-Free Diet

The Yeast-Free Diet has food restrictions that the other diets do not have. Therefore, it is necessary to begin with a list of yeast no-no's. To learn more about how yeast affects your body, see page 15.

DO NOT EAT OR DRINK

Alcoholic beverages
Barbecue sauce
Bread or hamburger buns
Buttermilk
Cake
Cashews
Catsup
Cheeses (except fresh)
Chili peppers
Citric acid
Dried roasted nuts
Fruit (especially dried and cured)
Horseradish
Mayonnaise
Malted products
Milk
Mincemeat
Mushrooms
Pastry
Peanuts
Pickles
Pistachios
Pretzels
Rolls
Root beer
Sauerkraut
Smoked foods
Sour cream
Soy sauce
Sugars of any type
Tomato sauce
Vitamins in a yeast base

This list may seem overwhelming. It is not! As you will see, this book is filled with wonderful recipes that will delight the taste buds and give a feeling of well-being.

Happily being faithful to this diet has very positive results. You will be able to overcome (with the help of supplements) your yeast sensitivity and once again enjoy—in moderation—foods containing yeast.

DAY 1

Breakfast

2–3 Eggs *Poached, *Hard or Soft Boiled
6 cooked shrimp
*Lemon Barbecue Sauce
Tea or decaffinated coffee with 1 tablespoon cream and sugar substitute

Lunch

*Gazpacho
Tuna fish with *Vinegar-Free Mayonnaise
2 1-gram crisp breads (GG is an example)
*Orange Cooler

Dinner

*Spicy Spareribs
Hearts of lettuce salad with *Tomato Mayonnaise Dressing
Sugar-free Jell-O

Snack

*Vanilla Ice Cream

DAY 2

Breakfast

*Scrambled or *Sunny-Side-Up and Over Easy eggs
3 slices boiled ham wrapped around a celery stick that is stuffed with cream cheese
Tea or decaffinated coffee with 1 tablespoon cream and sugar substitute

Lunch

*Brit Burger
½ cucumber, sliced, with minced fresh basil
*Shape-Up-Shake

Dinner

*Broiled Lobster Tails with Tarragon
*Crispy White Radish
Tossed green salad with *Creamy Celery Seed
Dressing made with *Vinegar-Free Mayonnaise
Tea or decaffinated coffee with 1 tablespoon cream and sugar substitute

Snack

*Hot Mint Chocolate Nog

DAY 3

Breakfast

Sliced steak sautéed in garlic butter
½ small onion, raw or sautéed in butter
2 slices *4 Grain and Seed Bread
Tea or decaffinated coffee with 1 tablespoon cream and sugar substitute

Lunch

*Luncheon Omelet

*Mocha Drink

Dinner

*Sardine snack on lettuce leaves
*Lemon-Basted Roast Chicken
Endive with *Lime Dill Dressing

Snack

*Black and White Ice Cream Soda

DAY 4

Breakfast

*Herb Omelet
2 slices *4 Grain and Seed Bread with cream cheese
*Cappuccino

Lunch

*Chicken Salad Ham Roll made with fresh ham (always use
*Vinegar-Free Mayonnaise)
*Blender-Thick Raspberry Shake

Dinner

*Japanese Egg Custard Soup (exclude mushrooms)
*Oriental Shrimp
*Raspberry Jell-O Cream
Tea or decaffinated coffee with 1 tablespoon cream and sugar
substitute

Snack

*Lemon Cream Jell-O

DAY 5

Breakfast

4 *Deviled-Salmon Egg halves
2 slices *Rye Bread with butter
*Spiced Iced Decaf Coffee

Lunch

*U.S. Hamburgers with *Tomato Mayonnaise
*Mock Potato Salad (exclude pickle)
Diet soda

Dinner

*Chicken Stock with *Dumplings
*Gourmet Game Hens
Tossed green salad with *Basic Vinegar-Free Salad Dressing
Tea or decaffinated coffee with 1 tablespoon cream and sugar substitute

Snack

*The 'Pop' Pop

DAY 6

Breakfast

*Ham and Artichoke Omelet
2 slices *Rye Bread
Tea or decaffinated coffee with 1 tablespoon cream and sugar substitute

Lunch

*Chicken Croquettes
Tossed green salad with *Tomato Mayonnaise
*Raspberry Cream Jell-O
Diet soda

Dinner

*Klara's Eggplant Appetizer on celery rounds
*Curry Crabmeat

Steamed broccoli
*Baked Cream
Tea or decaffinated coffee with 1 tablespoon cream and sugar substitute

Snack

Two *Brownie squares
Diet soda

DAY 7

Breakfast

*Salmon Soufflé
2 slices *4 Grain and Seed Bread
Tea and decaffinated coffee with 1 tablespoon cream and sugar substitute

Lunch

*Curry Burgers
Tossed green salad with *Lime Dill Dressing
2 *Almond Ball Cookies
Diet soda

Dinner

*Chicken Cacciatore with spaghetti squash
*String Beans Almandine
*Lemon-Lime Mousse
Tea or decaffinated coffee with 1 tablespoon cream and sugar substitute

Snack

½ cup *Decaf Coffee Ice Cream

The Maintenance Diet

When you have reached your ideal weight, you will begin Mainte-nance. At this level you may choose freely from any recipe in the book. And you may add back dried beans; all vegetables, including carrots, peas, beets, potatoes, sweet potatoes; all the sweet winter squash and plantains. Grains are permitted on the Maintainece Level. Actually, you will be eating a very healthy diet. That is the good news.

Sugars of all types are excluded from all of our diets. Although some of you may think they taste good, sugars are destructive to your health. Therefore, sugars—including honey, molasses, maple sugar and syrup, fructose, beet sugar, barley malt sugar, glucose, maltose, dextrose, corn syrup, sorbitol, mannitol, and hexitol—still are and will always be the bad news.

We encourage you to eat more protein than carbohydrates, unless the condition of your health does not permit it. Please drink 6 to 8 glasses of water a day and see a nutritionist who can help you with a vitamin program specific to your needs. When this becomes your life-style, you will be the slim, healthy, and energetic person that you always aspired to be.

The Yeast-Free Maintenance Diet

This diet is much the same as the Maintenance Diet. However, on this diet you will restrict cheeses, vinegars, and all fermented foods as well as sugar. In addition, you may wish to ask for yeast-free products at your health food store.

4 | *Recipes*

Eggs

Eggs are the perfect protein and we recommend them, especially **free range, organic eggs** (available in health food stores). In the New York area, these high-quality eggs are in supermarkets. The chickens that lay these eggs have not been injected with antibiotics or hormones and have not been fed chemicals. Always check the date on the box to ensure that the eggs are fresh.

You know that I don't have to tell you how to cook eggs. You have been cooking them for years. But I'd like to share some hints that have helped me. With any luck they may make your egg dishes even better than your usual great!

Separating An Egg:

Egg whites will not beat stiff if one drop of yolk gets mixed with the white when you separate the eggs. You can remove a small drop of yolk from white by using the cracked egg shell. Just dip it into the white and remove the yolk.

Beating Egg Whites:

To get the most volume from egg whites, bring them to room temperature before beating. They may be beaten with a wire whisk in a large metal bowl, a rotary beater, or an electric mixer. The electric mixer is most practical. Since egg whites lose volume quickly, beat them just before you need them.

Adding a pinch of cream of tartar to the unbeaten whites will help them sustain stiffness.

When adding beaten whites to a recipe, fold them in with a rubber spatula being careful not to break them down.

Using Egg Yolks as Thickeners:

This book uses egg yolks to thicken sauces, ice creams, and soufflés. Two egg yolks are equal to 1 tablespoon of flour or thickener. Beat eggs in a separate bowl and add ¼ cup of sauce to be thickened to the bowl. Beat together well. When eggs are blended with sauce, add egg mixture to sauce—stirring constantly over a low flame until sauce thickens. Do not boil sauce or egg yolk will scramble and sauce will become lumpy.

Soft-Boiled Eggs

1 serving

2 large eggs at room temperature
cold water to cover

Purchase a device called an "egg pricker" and put a small hole in the large end of the egg. This keeps eggs from cracking during cooking. Place eggs in water and bring to a boil. Boil for 3 minutes for loose eggs, 4 minutes for runny yolks and firmed whites, and 5 minutes for formed yolks and whites. Run under cold water to stop cooking. Crack open tops and serve in egg cups.

GRAMS PER SERVING 0.6

Hard-Boiled Eggs

1 serving

2 large eggs at room temperature
cold water to cover

Prick broad side of the egg. Place eggs in water. Bring water to a boil. Cover egg pan and turn off heat. Allow eggs to remain in water for 20 minutes. Refrigerate to cool.

GRAMS PER SERVING 0.6

How to Tell if an Egg Is Hard Boiled:
   Hard-boiled eggs will spin in their shells. Eggs that have not been cooked will not spin.

Scrambled Eggs

1 serving

2 eggs
1 tablespoon heavy cream
1 tablespoon sweet butter
salt and pepper to taste

Break eggs into a small bowl. Add cream and beat well with a wire whisk. Melt butter in a nonstick skillet, then add eggs. Cook on a low heat until eggs set. Season with salt and pepper (you may add other seasonings). When eggs set "scramble" them with a fork. Slide out of skillet and enjoy.
Variation: Sprinkle grated cheese over set eggs before scrambling.

GRAMS PER SERVING   2.0

Sunny-Side-Up and Over Easy

1 serving

2 eggs
1 tablespoon sweet butter
salt and pepper to taste

Melt butter in nonstick skillet. Break eggs, one at a time, into a flat saucer and slide them into the pan. Cook on a low heat until whites become solidly white and center is runny. Spoon melted butter over eggs while they cook. If Sunny-Side-Up is your way, remove from pan to plate after about 2½ minutes. For Over Easy, use a spatula and carefully flip eggs over. Cook for 30 seconds more. Salt and pepper to taste.

GRAMS PER SERVING   2.0

Poached Eggs

1 serving

2 eggs at room temperature
salt and pepper to taste

Fill skillet halfway with water and heat to a simmer. Break eggs one at a time into a flat saucer. Slide one into the simmering water, then slide the second in. Allow to simmer for 3 minutes until whites are no longer transparent. Remove from water with a slotted spoon. Place on a plate, season with salt and pepper and enjoy.

GRAMS PER SERVING   1.0

Cheese-Baked Eggs

1 serving

2 tablespoons grated Parmesan cheese
2 teaspoons sweet butter
2 tablespoons heavy cream
salt and pepper to taste

Preheat oven 375° F.

Fill a baking dish halfway with water and heat to a simmer. Place 1 teaspoon butter each in the bottom of 2 custard cups. Divide 1 tablespoon of cheese in the 2 cups. Carefully break an egg into each cup. Place 1 tablespoon of cream over each egg. Top with remaining cheese. Place custard cups in baking pan and set in the oven. Bake for 10 minutes. Salt and pepper to taste.

GRAMS PER SERVING   2.5

Basic Omelet

2 servings

2 tablespoons butter
4 eggs
1 tablespoon heavy cream
½ teaspoon seasoned salt
freshly cracked pepper to taste

Melt butter in a nonstick skillet or omelet pan. Tilt pan to cover well with butter.

Beat eggs with cream, salt, and pepper. Pour into pan and tilt pan to spread eggs to edges of pan.

Cook over a low flame until eggs begin to set. Loosen eggs from sides of pan with a spatula. Tilt pan again to allow uncooked eggs to run to the sides. Carefully fold outer edges of omelet into the center to resemble a flat cone. Slide omelet out of pan and serve.

When filling omelet, spoon mixture onto center of omelet before folding edges into the center.

TOTAL GRAMS   0.7
GRAMS PER SERVING   0.35

Bacon and Onion Omelet

6 servings

9 strips bacon
¼ cup diced onion
1 Basic Omelet *recipe*

Cut bacon into small pieces. Fry in small skilet. Add onion and sauté until all fat melts off bacon. Pour off fat. Follow recipe for *Basic Omelet*, above.

Place bacon and onion in center of omelet before folding over. Fold over and cook 1 minute. Serve immediately.

TOTAL GRAMS   10.1
GRAMS PER SERVING   1.7

Cheese-Tease Omelet

4 servings

8 eggs
½ cup creamed cottage cheese
½ cup cream cheese, softened
pinch salt
2 packets sugar substitute
1 teaspoon vanilla
½ teaspoon cinnamon
¼ cup heavy cream
3 tablespoons butter
2 tablespoons sour cream (optional)

Combine all ingredients except butter and sour cream in a bowl and beat until smooth.

Melt butter in a large nonstick omelet pan. Follow recipe for *Basic Omelet.*

Slide out of pan and serve plain or with sour cream on the side.

TOTAL GRAMS 1.1
GRAMS PER SERVING 4.2

Peaches and Cream Omelet

10 servings

1 8-ounce package cream cheese, softened
8 eggs
pinch salt
¼ cup heavy cream
1 packet Equal
2 tablespoons butter
⅓ cup Stewed Peaches, *chopped*

Combine all ingredients except butter and chopped peaches in a bowl and beat until smooth.

Follow recipe for *Basic Omelet.*

When center is firm, spoon peaches onto the center.
Slide out of pan and serve.

TOTAL GRAMS   51.0
GRAMS PER SERVING   5.1

Eggplant and Cheddar Omelet

4 servings

1 cup eggplant
4 tablespoons virgin olive oil
¼ teaspoon garlic powder (or 1 clove garlic, chopped)
½ cup tomato sauce
8 eggs
½ teaspoon seasoned salt
½ cup feta cheese

Peel eggplant. Cut into small cubes and soak in a bowl of cold water
for ½ hour. Dry eggplant well.

Place 3 tablespoons of olive oil into skillet. Add eggplant and
garlic. Sauté until eggplant begins to brown. Add tomato sauce. Set
aside.

Heat 1 tablespoon oil in large skillet. Add eggs and continue to
cook over low heat until they set.

Spoon eggplant mixture onto eggs and either fold it over or roll it
up.

TOTAL GRAMS   18.7
GRAMS PER SERVING   4.7

Herb Omelet

2 servings

4 eggs
1 tablespoon chopped chives
1 tablespoon minced dill
2 tablespoons mascarpone cheese
2 tablespoons butter
seasoned salt to taste

Combine all ingredients. Beat egg mixture well. Add seasoned salt.
   Follow directions for *Basic Omelet*.

TOTAL GRAMS 5.3
GRAMS PER SERVING 2.7

Eggs Florentine

6 servings

2 cups cooked fresh spinach (or 1 package frozen spinach)
6 eggs
seasoned salt to taste
1 recipe Cheese Sauce

Preheat oven to 350° F.
   Cooked spinach. Drain well. Chop fine.
   Place hot spinach in shallow baking dish.
   Make hole for each egg in spinach. Break egg into each hole with
salt.
   Prepare cheese sauce. Pour over eggs and spinach. Bake for 25
minutes.

TOTAL GRAMS 20.1
GRAMS PER SERVING   3.4

Salmon Soufflé

6 servings

2 tablespoons butter
3 tablespoons soy flour
1 teaspoon seasoned salt
1 cup heavy cream, heated
1 cup salmon, poached or canned
seasoned salt and cayenne pepper to taste
3 eggs, separated
1⅓ tablespoons lemon juice

Preheat oven to 400° F.

Prepare soufflé dish by rubbing inside with 1 tablespoon of butter. Place in refrigerator until ready to use.

Melt butter and stir in flour and salt. Whisk vigorously for 1 full minute to avoid floury taste. Add heated cream and cook over low heat, whisking, until thickened. Remove from heat and cool.

Add salmon, salt, and cayenne. Beat egg yolks, and blend them into the mixture.

Fold in stiffened beaten egg whites and lemon juice. Pour mixture into soufflé dish.

Set in a pan filled with 3 inches of hot water, and bake about 35 minutes until firm. Serve immediately.

TOTAL GRAMS 37.2
GRAMS PER SERVING 5.2

Spicy Sausage Omelet

4 servings

½ pound spicy sausage, cut in bite-size pieces
1 clove garlic, minced
¼ cup olive oil
1 teaspoon seasoned salt
1 teaspoon caraway seeds
1 tablespoon tomato paste
2 drops Tabasco sauce
6 eggs, beaten
1 tablespoon grated Parmesan cheese

Preheat oven to 325° F.

Sauté sausage and garlic in olive oil until sausage is well browned. Drain off fat. Add salt, caraway seeds, tomato paste, and Tabasco sauce. Stir well. Cool. Combine eggs and Parmesan cheese. Spoon meat mixture into baking dish and cover with eggs. Bake for 45 minutes or until set.

TOTAL GRAMS   12.0
GRAMS PER SERVING   3.0

Luncheon Omelet

4 servings

2 tablespoons olive oil
6 shiitake mushrooms
4 scallions, minced
12 snap peas
2 slices sun-dried tomatoes, diced
6 eggs
2 tablespoons heavy cream
1 tablespoon fresh dill, minced (½ tablespoon dried)
2 tablespoons sweet butter
2 ounces herbed goat cheese
salt and pepper to taste

Heat olive oil in a skillet. Sauté mushrooms and scallions for 2 minutes. Add snap peas and sun-dried tomatoes. Cook for 3 minutes (snap peas will remain crunchy).

Whisk eggs with cream and dill. Heat a nonstick omelet pan and melt butter in pan. Pour egg mixture into the pan. Follow directions for *Basic Omelet*.

TOTAL GRAMS 38.2
GRAMS PER SERVING 9.6

Two-Cheese Omelet

2 servings

2 tablespoons sweet butter
2 tablespoons onion, minced
4 eggs
2 tablespoons heavy cream
½ cup each of two cheeses, grated
1 tablespoon chopped parsley

This omelet is delicious when you choose one hard and one soft cheese such as cream cheese and Cheddar or Camembert and Parmesan. Use the soft cheese to mix with the egg mixture and the hard cheese in the center of the omelet.

Heat butter in a nonstick skillet. Add onion and cook until transparent. Beat eggs with heavy cream and soft cheese. Pour into pan. Spread egg mixture by tilting pan. Cook over low heat until eggs set. Sprinkle grated hard cheese in pan. Cook 1 minute. Slice egg pancake in two. Fold each semicircle in half. Flip over to melt cheese and brown both sides. Serve hot and crisp.

TOTAL GRAMS 8.2
GRAMS PER SERVING 4.1

Crabmeat and Mushroom Omelet

6 servings

2 tablespoons butter
6 shiitake mushrooms, thinly sliced
½ cup crabmeat
1 tablespoon sherry
6 eggs
3 tablespoons heavy cream

Melt butter in nonstick skillet. Add mushrooms and onion and sauté until light brown. Stir in crabmeat.

Simmer for 3 minutes. Add sherry and simmer 1 minute more.

Beat Eggs and cream together.

Follow *Basic Omelet* recipe.

Spoon half mixture over half of omelet just before folding, and place remaining mixture over top of omelet after it has been folded.

TOTAL GRAMS 12.0
GRAMS PER SERVING 2.0

Ham and Artichoke Omelet

2 servings

1 6-ounce jar marinated artichoke hearts
2 tablespoons grated Parmesan chesse
8 eggs
3 tablespoons mascarpone cheese
seasoned salt and pepper to taste
¼ pound ham, thinly sliced

Use a large nonstick omelet pan.

Place artichoke hearts on paper towel and pat oil off. Roll hearts in Parmesan cheese. Set aside. Beat eggs, mascarpone cheese, and salt and pepper together in a bowl. Follow the *Basic Omelet* instructions. When egg mixture is set, cover surface with ham slices. Place artichoke hearts into center and fold sides in. Slice in four pieces before removing from pan.

TOTAL GRAMS   20.7
GRAMS PER SERVING   5.2

Shrimp and Goat Cheese Omelet

2 servings

8 raw shrimp, cleaned and butterflied
4 tablespoons garlic oil
2 tablespoons sweet butter
4 eggs
2 ounces herbed goat cheese, roughly grated
4 sun-dried tomato halves softened in olive oil and minced

Use a 9-inch nonstick skillet or omelet pan.

Butterfly shrimp by cutting ¾ of the way through—along the back vein. Open shrimp to resemble a butterfly.

Sear the shrimp in hot garlic oil (about 2 minutes on each side). Remove to paper toweling. Wipe oil from pan with a paper towel.

Add butter to pan. Beat eggs with goat cheese and follow directions for *Basic Omelet.*

When eggs are set, place shrimp and sun-dried tomatoes on egg pancake and fold over.

TOTAL GRAMS   14.0
GRAMS PER SERVING   6.9

Appetizers

Marbleized Tea Eggs From China

12 hors d'oeuvres

6 eggs
2 tablespoons soy sauce
2 tablespoons salt
3 tablespoons black tea
1 tablespoon anise extract

Cover eggs with cold water and bring to a boil. Simmer 10 minutes.

Remove eggs, cool, and crack the shells in several places, but do not peel.

Bring 4 cups of water to a boil. Add remaining ingredients and eggs. Simmer for one hour. Cool.

Place eggs still in the water in the refrigerator. Leave overnight.

To serve, shell eggs and cut in half. They are very attractive on the hors d'oeuvres tray.

TOTAL GRAMS   2.3
GRAMS PER SERVING   0.2

Deviled-Salmon Eggs

12 egg halves

6 eggs
3 tablespoons mayonnaise
½ cup boned and flaked salmon, canned or smoked
½ teaspoon lemon juice
1 teaspoon prepared mustard
1 teaspoon Worcestershire sauce
½ teaspoon salt
dash of pepper

Gently boil eggs for 15 minutes. Turn often to help keep yolks in center. Run eggs under cold water and remove shells. Slice eggs in half lengthwise. Flatten bottom of egg whites by cutting a small slice off bottom side. Remove yolks.

Mash yolks and mayonnaise together until smooth. Add remaining ingredients (reserve enough salmon for garnish) and mix well.

Spoon mixture into egg whites.

Garnish with pieces of salmon. Refrigerate for at least ½ hour.

TOTAL GRAMS 4.0
GRAMS PER HALF EGG 0.3

Swedish Meatballs

30 meatballs

¼ cup heavy cream
¼ cup water
¼ cup fried pork rinds, * *crushed*
¼ pound beef, ground
¼ pound pork, ground
¼ pound veal, ground
1 large onion, chopped fine
3 tablespoons butter
2 teaspoons seasoned salt
½ recipe Cream Sauce
nutmeg
caraway seeds

Mix heavy cream and water together. Add crushed pork rinds and allow to soak. Combine beef, pork, and veal.

Sauté onion in 1 tablespoon butter until lightly brown. Mix cream mixture, meat, and onion together. Add seasoned salt. Shape into small balls, and brown in 2 tablespoons butter.

Remove balls to chafing dish and keep warm.

Make *Cream Sauce* and pour over meatballs. Garnish with nutmeg and caraway seeds.

TOTAL GRAMS 16.3
GRAMS PER MEATBALL 0.5

Turkey Meatballs

8 meatballs

2 tablespoons butter
1 small onion, minced
1 medium stalk of celery, minced
1 clove garlic, minced

---

*Sugar-Free

½ pound turkey, ground
1 teaspoon seasoned salt
¼ teaspoon pepper
1 tablespoon grated Parmesan cheese
½ teaspoon thyme
1 egg
¼ teaspoon curry powder

Heat butter in a small skillet. Sauté onion, celery, and garlic until golden brown.

Place turkey in a bowl, add onion mixture and remaining ingredients. Mix lightly with a fork. Shape into 1-inch balls and sauté. Serve with a toothpick.

TOTAL GRAMS 29.6
GRAMS PER MEATBALL 3.7

Salami and Parmesan

8 cubes

½ pound salami, cut into eight cubes
2 eggs, beaten
4 tablespoons grated Parmesan cheese
walnut oil for frying

Dip salami into beaten eggs and then coat with Parmesan cheese. Repeat.

Fry in deep hot oil for 30 seconds.

TOTAL GRAMS 4.0
GRAMS PER SERVING 0.5

Heavenly Wings

Hors d'oeuvres for 6

1½ pounds chicken wings
1 cup Tamari soy sauce
4 packets sugar substitute
¼ cup white wine
2 cloves garlic, mashed
¼ cup oil
½ teaspoon ground ginger

Preheat oven to 325° F.

Wash wings and pat dry. Cut into pieces at joints. Discard wing tips. Combine ingredients for sauce.

Spread wings in shallow baking dish. Do not overlap. Pour sauce over wings. Marinate overnight in refrigerator. Bake in marinade for 1½ hours.

TOTAL GRAMS 17.4
GRAMS PER SERVING 3.0

Sardine Snack

3 snacks

1 can skinless and boneless sardines, drained
½ teaspoon dried parsley
¼ teaspoon dill weed
3 hard-boiled eggs, mashed
¼ teaspoon salt
6 ounces cream cheese, mashed
2 tablespoons chopped onion
¾ teaspoon lemon juice

Combine all ingredients in a blender or food processor. Blend until smooth. Serve on bed of lettuce leaves.

TOTAL GRAMS 6.0
GRAMS PER SERVING 2.0

Sour Cream Clam Dip

8 servings

1 cup sour cream
1 7-ounce can minced clams, drained
½ cut chopped onion
2 teaspoons clam juice, from the can
1 tablespoon grated onion
1 teaspoon celery seed
¼ cup mayonnaise
1 tablespoon lemon juice
seasoned salt and pepper to taste

Mix all ingredients together well.
  Refrigerate for at least 1 hour. Serve with fried pork rinds.

TOTAL GRAMS 16.4
GRAMS PER SERVING 2.2

Guacamole

8 ¼-cup servings

1 avocado, peeled and chopped
½ cup onion, chopped
1 tomato, chopped
½ cucumber, peeled and chopped
½ teaspoon paprika
½ teaspoon seasoned salt
1 jalapeño pepper, minced
⅛ teaspoon hot chili pepper, dried
1 tablespoon sour cream
1 tablespoon chopped parsley

Place avocado, onion, tomato, and cucumber in bowl and chop together. Season with paprika, salt, and peppers. Add sour cream and parsley. Refrigerate. Use as dip with sliced cucumbers.

TOTAL GRAMS 31.0
GRAMS PER SERVING 4.0

Fran's Special Pâté

20 slices

4 slices no-nitrate bacon
1 pound chicken livers
1 chicken cutlet, pounded flat
4 teaspoons seasoned salt
3 tablespoons bacon fat
2 tablespoons butter
2 tablespoons white wine
½ 8-ounce can water chestnuts
2 hard-boiled eggs
1 Boursin cheese
3 tablespoons sweet basil
freshly ground black pepper

Preheat oven to 275° F.

Cook bacon until crisp. Reserve fat.

Place 2 tablespoons of bacon fat in frying pan. Sauté chicken livers until they are pink inside.

Season chicken cutlet with 1 teaspoon salt, and sauté in butter for 3 minutes on each side. Add wine and simmer for 5 minutes. Reserve sauce.

Put bacon, chicken livers, chicken, water chestnuts, and eggs into a large wooden chopping bowl or food processor and chop fine.

Add remaining seasoned salt, Boursin cheese, basil, chicken sauce, and pepper. Mix well. Pack into a large buttered loaf pan. Place a heavy weight on top to keep pâté from rising.

Bake for 2 hours. Open oven door and bake for 1 hour more.

Remove from oven and allow to come to room temperature. Refrigerate.

TOTAL GRAMS 32.0
GRAMS PER SERVING 1.6

Cheesy Ham Snack

6 servings

1 tablespoon of mayonnaise
1 tablespoon grated Parmesan cheese
6 slices black forest ham
6 thin slices Swiss cheese
1 small tomato, sliced thin

Mix mayonnaise with Parmesan cheese.

Spread mixture on slice of ham, top with tomato slices. Roll up. Place ham roll on a thin slice of Swiss cheese and roll again. Fasten with toothpick.

TOTAL GRAMS 27.1
GRAMS PER SERVING 4.5

Caribbean Crabmeat

30 canapés

2 tablespoons butter
2 tablespoons onion
1 clove galic
½ cup grated coconut, unsweetened
2 cups crabmeat, fresh or canned
1 egg
2 tablespoons cream
2 teaspoons curry powder
1 teaspoon salt
½ cup fried pork rinds, crushed
½ cup oil

Melt 2 tablespoons butter in skillet. Sauté onion and garlic until transparent.

Add coconut to skillet and sauté until light brown.

Combine crabmeat, egg, cream, curry powder, and salt. Add onion and garlic mixture and coconut. Mix well.

Shape into 1-inch balls. Roll in pork rinds. Heat oil in skillet. Brown crabmeat balls in hot oil. Drain thoroughly on absorbent paper. Serve on toothpicks.

TOTAL GRAMS   23.8
GRAMS PER SERVING   0.6

Klara's Eggplant Appetizer

6 servings

1 medium eggplant
1 medium onion, sliced
1 tablespoon extra-virgin olive oil
1 teaspoon balsamic vinegar
¼ teaspoon seasoned salt
pepper to taste

Preheat oven to 350° F. Bake eggplant for 1 hour. Remove skin while still hot. Cool. Chop all ingredients together.

TOTAL GRAMS   16.8
GRAMS PER SERVING   2.8

JELL-O SNACKS

Snappy Raspberry and Lemons

4 ½-cup servings

1 package sugar-free raspberry Jell-O
1 cup boiling water
1 cup cold diet Snapple raspberry iced tea

Dissolve Jell-O in hot water. Cool. Add iced tea. Refrigerate until jelled.
     For lemon, use lemon Jell-O and diet Snapple lemon iced tea.

TOTAL GRAMS   0.5
GRAMS PER SERVING   0.1

Raspberry or Lemon Jell-O Cream

8 ½-cup servings

1 package sugar-free raspberry Jell-O
1 cup diet Snapple raspberry iced tea, heated to boiling
1 cup sour cream

Disolve Jell-O in hot Snapple. Cool to room temperature.

Whisk in sour cream, beating until blended. Refrigerate until jelled.

For lemon cream, use diet lemon Jell-O and diet Snapple lemon iced tea.

TOTAL GRAMS   10.2
GRAMS PER SERVING   1.3

Tomato, Lemon Jell-O

4 ½-cup servings

½ cup water, boiling
1 package sugar-free lemon Jell-O
1½ cups Piquant V-8 Juice, chilled

Bring water to a boil. Dissolve Jell-O in water. Cool.

Add V-8 and chill until firm.

TOTAL GRAMS   0.8
GRAMS PER SERVING   0.2

Strawberry-Banana Cream

4 ½-cup servings

1 cup water
1 teaspoon banana extract
1 package sugar-free strawberry-banana Jell-O

2 tablespoons No-Cal strawberry syrup
½ cup diet strawberry soda
6 tablespoons heavy cream

Heat water to a boil. Add banana extract. Pour over Jell-O and completely dissolve it. Cool. Add syrup, soda, and cream. Whisk until well blended. Refrigerate until firm.

TOTAL GRAMS   2.4
GRAMS PER SERVING   0.6

Toasted Nuts

½ cup toasted nuts

1 teaspoon butter
½ cup nuts of your choice

Melt butter in non-stick pan. Stir in nuts and sauté until lightly browned.

Place on paper toweling to absorb excess oil.
If you like them salty, use seasoned salt to taste.
If you like them sweet, use a sugar substitute to taste.
If you like them spicy, use chili powder to taste.

TOTAL GRAMS FOR TOASTED ALMONDS   20.0
TOTAL GRAMS FOR TOASTED WALNUTS   12.4
TOTAL GRAMS FOR TOASTED PECANS   8.4
TOTAL GRAMS FOR TOASTED PINE NUTS   16.0

Soups

These four stocks are important to many of the recipes in this book. Stocks are soups that have been strained. They freeze easily and safely. I freeze them in small containers (no more than two cups) so they can be defrosted quickly. Once you've tried these stocks, their value will be apparent. Every recipe will taste much more zesty and flavorful as a result of using them.

Chicken Stock

8 1-cup servings

1 4–5 pound chicken, cleaned and washed
3 quarts cold water
1 teaspoon seasoned salt
2 stalks celery (or 1 cup)
1 tablespoon parsley
1 small onion, chopped
1 parsnip, diced
1 bay leaf
1 pinch of thyme
1 Knorr chicken boullion cube

Place cleaned chicken in cold water. Bring to a boil. Remove foam that forms on top of water.

Add remaining ingredients.

Cover and simmer chicken until it is tender (about 1½ hours).

Cool. Remove chicken and strain stock. Chill the stock in a covered container in refrigerator.

Remove layer of fat that will rise to the top when thoroughly chilled.

Heat stock for soup and sauces. Or use it cold to make an aspic or jellied soup.

The chicken and vegetables may be returned to stock for a chicken soup meal or use chicken to make *Chicken Salad*.

TOTAL GRAMS 20.4
GRAMS PER SERVING 2.7

Cream of Chicken Soup

1 serving

1 cup Chicken Stock
2 tablespoons heavy cream
1 egg yolk (for thickening)

Whisk cream and yolk into hot stock. Simmer 1 minute. Do not boil!

TOTAL GRAMS 0.8

Vegetable Stock

8 1-cup servings

2 tablespoons butter
2 sprigs fresh parsley (or 1 teaspoon dried parsley flakes)
1 large onion, sliced
1 large carrot, sliced
3 stalks celery, sliced
2 quarts water
6 whole peppercorn
2 whole cloves
1 bay leaf
2 tablespoons wine vinegar (optional)

Melt butter in deep saucepan over medium flame. Add vegetables and sauté for 5 minutes. Add water and seasonings, cover tightly, and simmer for 30 minutes.

Strain and use as directed in recipes.

TOTAL GRAMS 18.9
GRAMS PER SERVING 2.3

Beef Stock

8 1-cup servings

2 pounds beef stew meat
1 teaspoon salt
3 quarts cold water
¼ teaspoon pepper
¼ cup onion, diced
¼ cup carrot, diced
¼ cup celery, diced
¼ cup tomato, diced
1 teaspoon parsley, chopped
1 teaspoon green pepper, chopped

Place meat and salt in cold water, and bring to a boil over low heat. Skim bubbles off the top. Cover and simmer for 2½ hours.

Add the vegetables, seasonings, and pepper and cook slowly for an additional 1½ hours.

Remove meat and serve with horseradish or mustard sauce. Strain stock and use as directed in recipes.

TOTAL GRAMS 6.3
GRAMS PER SERVING 0.7

Fish Stock

6 1-cup servings

2 pounds fish trimmings
2 quarts water
2 cloves
½ teaspoon mace
3 stalks celery, with tops
1 parsley sprig
1 bay leaf
5 peppercorns
1 tablespoon salt

Place all ingredients in deep saucepan. Cover tightly and bring to a boil. Lower flame and simmer gently for 45 minutes. Strain, cool, and store in refrigerator. Use as directed in recipes.

TOTAL GRAMS   1.8
GRAMS PER SERVING   0.3

Dumplings

4 servings

1 tablespoon soft butter
1 egg plus 1 yolk
½ cup heavy cream
pinch of nutmeg
4 cups Chicken Stock

Spray top of double boiler with oil substitute. Rub with butter.

Beat eggs, heavy cream, salt, and nutmeg together with fork. Pour into top of double boiler.

Cook over hot (not boiling) water for 45 minutes, or until set and firm. Turn out onto waxed paper and cool. Slice into cubes. Add to clear hot stock. Serve immediately.

TOTAL GRAMS   5.3
GRAMS PER SERVING   1.3

Make stock into soup by adding these creamy delights:

Cream of Shiitake Mushroom Soup

10 servings

½ pound shiitake mushrooms, sliced thin
½ medium onion, minced
¼ pound butter
1 quart Chicken Stock
1 quart Beef Stock
2 tablespoons crushed toasted sesame seeds (crush in blender)
½ teaspoon seasoned salt
1 cup heavy cream
1 tablespoon chives, minced

Sauté mushrooms and onions in half butter for 5 minutes. Mix the stocks; add mushrooms and onions. Melt remaining butter in saucepan. Add crushed sesame seeds. Gradually add ¼ cup of stock, stirring steadily.

Return sesame mixture to balance of stock. Add salt. Cook over low heat for 10 minutes. Cool. Stir in heavy cream until well blended. Do not allow to boil.

Serve in cups garnished with chives.

TOTAL GRAMS 27.6
GRAMS PER SERVING 2.8

Creamy Ricotta Soup

6 servings

1 onion, chopped fine
1 stalk celery, chopped
2 green peppers, chopped
3 tablespoons butter
3 cups Vegetable Stock
1½ teaspoon seasoned salt
½ teaspoon paprika

2 cups ricotta cheese pushed through a strainer
4 sprigs parsley, minced
3 strips bacon, fried crisp

Sauté onion, celery, and peppers in butter. Heat vegetable stock in sauce pan. Add sautéed vegetables, seasoned salt, and paprika.

Cover and simmer gently for 1 hour. Add salt, pepper, and paprika. Cover and simmer gently for 1 hour.

Add ricotta cheese and put mixture in blender. Blend at medium speed until smooth.

Garnish with minced parsley and bacon pieces. Serve hot.

TOTAL GRAMS 28.4
GRAMS PER SERVING 4.7

Gazpacho

6 servings

¼ teaspoon garlic powder
1 onion, chopped
4 parsley sprigs
2 tablespoons vinegar
3 tablespoons olive oil
¼ teaspoon cayenne pepper
¼ teaspoon seasoned salt
1½ cups Chicken Stock
4 large tomatoes, peeled
2 tablespoons cucumber, diced
2 tablespoons green pepper, diced
2 tablespoons fried pork rinds, crushed

Place all ingredients except last 3 in blender or food processor. Blend until smooth. Chill overnight. Serve in chilled bowls. Garnish each with 1 teaspoon each cucumber, pepper, and crushed pork rinds.

TOTAL GRAMS 31.7
GRAMS PER SERVING 5.3

Cold Avocado Soup

6 servings

1½ cups avocado, diced and peeled
3 tablespoons lime juice
½ teaspoon salt
dash pepper
dash nutmeg
3 cups Chicken Stock
¼ cup heavy cream whipped

Place avocado, lime juice, salt, pepper, and nutmeg in a blender. Add ½ cup *Chicken Stock*. Blend 30 seconds at high speed. Pour into bowl.

Whisk in remaining broth and chill until icy cold.

Serve garnished with a spoonful of whipped cream and a sprinkle of nutmeg.

TOTAL GRAMS 30.6
GRAMS PER SERVING 5.1

Japanese Egg Custard Soup

6 servings

1 cup julienne-cut cooked chicken or diced shrimp
3 water chestnuts, diced
6 mushrooms, diced
2 scallions, chopped
1 tablespoon sherry
4 eggs, beaten
1 teaspoon salt
3 cups Beef Stock
12 spinach or lettuce leaves

Preheat oven to 300° F.

Combine chicken or shrimp, water chestnuts, mushrooms, scallions, and sherry. Divide sugar substitutely into 6 custard cups.

Beat eggs, salt, and stock together. Pour into custard cups. Cover with spinach or lettuce leaves.

Place in large pan with 3 inches boiling water. Cover pan and bake for 30 minutes or until mixture is set.

TOTAL GRAMS 5.3
GRAMS PER SERVING 1.3

New England Fish Chowder

6 servings

2 pounds cod fillets
4 slices bacon, diced
1 small onions, diced
2 tablespoons parsley, chopped
2 cups Fish Stock
1 bay leaf
1 teaspoon seasoned salt
2 cups heavy cream

Cut fish fillets into 1-inch cubes. Place bacon in deep saucepan over low heat and sauté until golden brown. Add onions and sauté until transparent. Add parsley and cook 1 minute more.

Add stock, bay leaf, salt, and pepper. Cover and cook for a few minutes to combine flavors. Add fish, and simmer for 10 minutes. Add cream and heat to the boiling point. Do not boil. Serve immediately.

TOTAL GRAMS 24.0
GRAMS PER SERVING 4.0

New England Clam Chowder

6 servings

Wash 3 dozen clams thoroughly. Steam in covered pot in 4–6 inches of boiling water until shells open (no longer than 5 minutes). Strain clam stock and use as part of water in recipe. Chop clams coarsely and substitute for cod fillets in *New England Fish Chowder* recipe (above).

TOTAL GRAMS 25.8
GRAMS PER SERVING 4.3

Baked Scallop and Fish Soup

4 servings

1 ounce sweet butter
1 large fish fillet, any variety
2 cloves garlic, minced
3 small ripe tomatoes, peeled and chopped
½ medium onion, chopped
10 shiitake mushrooms or any mushroom, sliced thin
½ cup pine nuts
1 pound of sea scallops
¼ cup white wine
1 tablespoon fresh dill, minced (or 2 teaspoons dried dill)

Preheat oven 350° F.
    Melt butter on bottom of a deep-sided baking dish.
    Place fish in dish and top with garlic. Add tomato, onion, mushrooms, nuts, and scallops. Sprinkle with wine. Cover and bake for 20 minutes. Remove cover and cook 10 minutes more. Place in soup bowls. Garnish with dill.

TOTAL GRAMS 62.5
GRAMS PER SERVING 15.6

Vichyssoise with Dill and Caraway

6 servings

2 tablespoons sweet butter
3 leeks (white part only), chopped
½ medium cauliflower, chopped
3 cups Chicken Stock
1 chicken bouillon cube
1 cup heavy cream
2 tablespoons dill, minced
2 tablespoons caraway seeds
1 packet sugar substitute
seasoned salt to taste
6 tablespoons mascarpone cheese
6 tablespoons grated Parmesan cheese

Melt butter in a medium-sized pot. Add leek and cauliflower and sauté for 3 minutes. Stir in *Chicken Stock* and bouillon cube. Cook over medium heat for ½ hour. Remove from heat. Cool. Place in food processor and blend. Add cream and blend 10 seconds more. Return to pan. Stir in fresh dill and caraway seeds. Warm to desired heat. Place in individual bowls. Top each with 1 tablespoon mascarpone and 1 tablespoon Parmesan. Serve hot.

TOTAL GRAMS   42.1
GRAMS PER SERVING   7.0

Salads

Chicken Salad Ham Rolls

4 servings

1 cup cooked chicken, diced
¼ cup mayonnaise
¼ cup chopped parsley
¼ cup chopped celery leaves
1 teaspoon seasoned salt
6 black olives, diced
4 tablespoons minced fresh green pepper
8 slices boiled ham
lettuce leaves

Combine all ingredients except ham and lettuce. Spread mixture on ham slices and roll each one up, insert toothpicks and place them seam side down on bed of lettuce leaves.

TOTAL GRAMS 16.6
GRAMS PER SERVING 4.2

Fresh Tuna and Avocado Salad

6 servings

1 large avocado, pitted, peeled, and cubed
2 stalks celery, chopped
6 radishes, sliced
4 tablespoons lemon juice
4 tablespoons tarragon vinegar
½ small onion, chopped
¼ teaspoon cayenne pepper
seasoned salt to taste
1½ pounds fresh tuna fish, grilled

Toss all ingredients together well, except fish.
   Cut fish in strips and place across top.
   Serve with *Dill Vinaigrette.*

TOTAL GRAMS   29.5
GRAMS PER SERVING   5.0

Cole Slaw

6 ½-cup servings

¼ cup Dijon mustard
¼ cup mayonnaise
½ packet sugar substitute
1 tablespoon lemon juice
½ teaspoon salt
1 medium cabbage, shredded (3 cups)

Mix mustard, mayonnaise, sugar substitite, lemon juice, and salt together. Add cabbage and toss well.

TOTAL GRAMS   41.4
GRAMS PER SERVING   7.0

A Mold of Roquefort

12 servings

1 envelope unflavored gelatin
¼ cup cold water
6 ounces Roquefort cheese
6 ounces cream cheese, softened
½ cup heavy cream
4 scallions, minced
2 tablespoons pine nuts
4 black olives, chopped
seasoned salt to taste

Sprinkle gelatin over water. Push Roquefort cheese through strainer. Add cream cheese and heavy cream to Roquefort cheese. Mix well. Add gelatin, scallions, pine nuts, olives, and salt to cheese mixture. Mix well.

Pour into 3-cup ring mold that has been sprayed with oil substitute. Chill. Occasionally stir gently until set.

TOTAL GRAMS 17.1
GRAMS PER SERVING 1.4

Mock Potato Salad

8 ½-cup servings

1 medium rutabaga
pot of boiling water
½ packet sugar substitute
1 tablespoon lemon juice
½ cup finely chopped scallions
1 medium dill pickle, chopped
1 cup minced celery with leaves
1½ teaspoon salt
dash of paprika
¾ cup mayonnaise
4 hard-boiled eggs, chopped

Pare rutabaga, and cut into 4 pieces. Drop into boiling water and boil until tender (about ½ hour). Drain well. Cool.

After rutabaga has cooled, dice (should be approximately 2½ cups), and place in salad bowl. Sprinkle with sugar substitute and lemon juice. Add scallions, pickle, celery, salt, paprika, and mayonnaise.

Toss well. Fold in eggs. Chill before serving.

TOTAL GRAMS 69.4
GRAMS PER SERVING 8.7

Tossed Salad with Tomato Dressing

12 servings

2 heads lettuce (any variety)
2 tomatoes
6 scallions
1 tablespoon dry mustard
½ teaspoon garlic powder
1 tablespoon Dijon mustard
1 teaspoon seasoned salt
2 tablespoons olive oil
2 tablespoons tarragon vinegar
4 tablespoons vegetable oil
1 tablespoon mayonnaise

Wash lettuce, dry thoroughly, and break into bite-size pieces. Refrigerate.

Tomato Dressing
Chop tomatoes and scallions together until mushy. Add all other ingredients except lettuce. Beat with wire whisk. Refrigerate.

When ready to serve, place lettuce in large salad bowl, pour dressing on top, and toss well. Serve immediately.

TOTAL GRAMS 42.5
GRAMS PER SERVING 3.5

Not Just Another Tossed Salad

12 servings

2 pounds large shrimp, deveined
½ cup garlic oil
½ pound fresh spinach, washed and dried
1 small head Boston lettuce, washed and dried
½ 7¼-ounce can large black olives, sliced
½ cup diced celery
5 scallions, diced
6 radishes, sliced
½ cup diced raw cauliflower florets
1 avocado, peeled and diced
8 slices bacon, crisp and crumbled
2 soft-boiled eggs (2 minutes)
½ cup lemon juice
¼ cup peanut oil
¼ cup grated Parmesan cheese
seasoned salt to taste

Sauté shrimp in garlic oil until they turn pink. Refrigerate while you prepare salad.

Break spinach and lettuce into bite-size pieces. Toss all vegetables and bacon together in bowl.

Make dressing by beating eggs, lemon juice, oil, cheese, and salt together.

Top salad with shrimp. Pour dressing over salad and serve.

TOTAL GRAMS 51.7
GRAMS PER SERVING 4.3

Greek Salad

6 servings

1 large tomato, cubed
½ large green pepper, cubed
½ large cucumber, pared and cubed
½ 6-ounce can ripe pitted olives
3 scallions, diced
2 tablespoons capers
¼ pound feta cheese, crumbled
12 thin slices pepperoni
4 tablespoons olive oil
2 tablespoons wine vinegar
¼ teaspoon cracked pepper
½ teaspoon oregano

Combine tomato, pepper, cucumber, olives, scallions, capers, cheese, and pepperoni in salad bowl. Mix olive oil, vinegar, pepper, and oregano together in small bowl. Pour dressing over vegetables. Toss and serve.

TOTAL GRAMS 25.0
GRAMS PER SERVING 4.1

Honeydew and Seafood

6 servings

1 1-pound honeydew melon
1 6½-ounce can tuna fish
1 4½-ounce can shrimp
1 medium cucumber, peeled and cubed
½ pound raw mushrooms, sliced
½ cup mayonnaise
2 tablespoons tomato sauce
½ teaspoon seasoned salt

Cut melon in half. Scoop out center and make balls. Leave rim ¼-inch wide. Cut into thirds.

In bowl combine tuna fish, shrimp (save a few for garnish), cucumber, mushrooms, and melon balls.

Combine mayonnaise, tomato sauce, and salt. Pour dressing over seafood. Mix well.

Fill melon shells. Garnish with some shrimp.

If you prefer low fat, eliminate dressing, and use juice of 1 lemon.

TOTAL GRAMS 44.4
GRAMS PER SERVING 7.3

Chicken Salad

2 servings

2 cups chicken meat (from Chicken Stock*)*
⅓ cup marinated artichoke hearts, drained
20 black olives
3 tablespoons onion, minced
1 tablespoon sweet butter
2 tablespoons crème fraîche or sour cream
1 tablespoon mayonnaise
seasoned salt to taste

Toss first 5 ingredients together. Mix créme frâiche and mayonnaise together. Add to chicken mixture. Mix well. Season with salt.
Refrigerate.

TOTAL GRAMS 8.6
GRAMS PER SERVING 4.3

Poached Salmon Salad

2 servings

whole leaves of 1 endive
1 small tomato, peeled and quartered
1 small ripe avocado, peeled
¼ small onion, diced (Vidalia when possible)
6 pitted black olives
2 salmon fillets, poached
1 recipe Lime Dill Dressing

Wash and dry endive leaves. Chop tomato, avocado, onion, and olives together in a wooden chopping bowl. Poach salmon and allow it to come to room temperature.

Place endive leaves in a daisy formation in a round, shallow salad bowl. Make chopped tomato mixture the center of the daisy. Place strips of salmon in each of the endive leaves. Artistically dot with *Lime Dill Dressing.*

TOTAL GRAMS 39.8
GRAMS PER SERVING 19.9

Hot Beef Salad

6 servings

1 small head Boston lettuce
1 small Chinese cabbage
1 large cucumber, sliced thin
1 red onion, peeled and sliced thin
½ small daikon radish, sliced thin
2 small tomatoes, cut in eight pieces
6 mint leaves
6 coriander leaves
¼ cup walnut oil
1½ pound sirloin, sliced thin
½ teaspoon seasoned salt

Dressing
5 garlic cloves, minced
¼ cup fresh lime juice
1 packet sugar substitite
1 tablespoon Tamari soy sauce
2 teaspoons crushed red pepper flakes
¼ cup sharp Cheddar cheese, diced

Wash and dry lettuce and cabbage. Rip into bite-sized pieces. Mix onions, radishes, tomatoes, and mint and coriander leaves together with oil and pour over lettuce. Toss.

Heat oil in a nonstick skillet over medium heat. Add meat and seasoned salt. Cook quickly, stirring frequently.

Artfully arrange cooked meat on salad. Mix dressing ingredients together and pour over salad. Top with Cheddar cubes.

TOTAL GRAMS   67.0
GRAMS PER SERVING   11.5

Leftover Lamb or Pork Salad

2 servings

1 pound leftover lamb or pork
seasoned salt to taste
pepper to taste
3 tablespoons extra-virgin olive oil
2 tablespoons fresh rosemary, minced
1 tablespoon balsamic vinegar
1 teaspoon Dijon mustard
2 heads Bibb lettuce, cored, washed, and dried
¼ cup Parmesan cheese shavings

Thinly slice lamb or pork. Whisk together salt, pepper, oil, rosemary, vinegar, and mustard.

Place greens in a salad bowl with Parmesan shavings and toss them with the dressing. Arrange meat over greens.

TOTAL GRAMS   11.2
GRAMS PER SERVING   5.6

Salad Niçoise with Fresh Tuna

12 servings

2 teaspoons Dijon mustard
2 tablespoons wine vinegar
1½ teaspoons salt
2 cloves garlic, minced
6 tablespoons peanut or vegetable oil
6 tablespoons olive oil
Freshly ground black pepper
1 teaspoon chopped fresh thyme (or ½ teaspoon dried)
2 pounds green beans
2 green peppers
4 celery stalks
1 pint cherry tomatoes
3 7-ounce cans tuna
1 2-ounce can flat anchovies
10 stuffed green olives
10 black olives
2 small or l large red onion
2 tablespoons chopped fresh basil (or 1 teaspoon dried)
⅓ cup finely chopped fresh parsley
¼ cup finely chopped scallions
6 hard-boiled eggs, quartered

Combine mustard, vinegar, salt, garlic, peanut and olive oil, pepper, and thyme in a bowl. Beat with a fork until well blended. Set aside.

Pick over beans and break into 1½-inch lengths. Place beans in a saucepan and cook, in salted water to cover, until crisp-tender. Run under cold water and drain in a colander. Set aside.

Remove cores, seeds, and white membranes from green peppers. Cut peppers in thin rounds. Set aside.

Trim celery stalks and cut crosswise into thin slices. Set aside.

Bring a quart of water to a boil. Drop in cherry tomatoes and let stand for exactly 15 seconds. Drain immediately. Pull off tomato skins with a paring knife. Set tomatoes aside.

Use a large salad bowl and make a more or less symmetrical pattern of the green beans, peppers, celery, and tomatoes. Flake the tuna fish and add to bowl. Arrange anchovies on top and scatter olives over all.

Peel onions and cut them into thin, almost transparent slices. Scatter onion rings over all. Sprinkle with basil, parsley, and scallions. Garnish with eggs.

Toss salad with dressing just before serving.

TOTAL GRAMS 127.2
GRAMS PER SERVING 10.6

Crunchy Seafood Salad

10 servings

1 6½-ounce can tuna fish
1 6-ounce can crabmeat
1 5-ounce can shrimp
1 large head lettuce
1 cup diced celery
½ cup diced green onions
½ medium ripe avocado, diced
½ cup chopped walnuts
½ cup roasted unsalted soybeans
½ cup sunflower seeds
2 hard-boiled eggs, diced
1 tomato cut in wedges

Drain the 3 cans of seafood, discard bony tissue from crab, and devein shrimp. Place in a bowl and refrigerate.

Combine remaining ingredients except tomato, in a large salad bowl, and toss well.

Add seafood and toss again.

Add salad dressing of your choice.

Toss again before serving, and decorate with tomato wedges.

TOTAL GRAMS 77.0
GRAMS PER SERVING 7.7

Tricolor Salad with Three Cheeses

8 servings

1 recipe Mustard Vinaigrette
1 small head of radicchio
3 endive
1 head of romaine
3 ounces Parmesan cheese shavings
5 ounces of Camembert, cut into 8 wedges
4 ounces herbed goat cheese, cut into 8 wedges
¼ cup pine nuts, toasted (or substitute Toasted Nuts*)*

Preheat oven to 450° F.

Prepare vinaigrette and place in refrigerator for ½ hour. Separate lettuce leaves. Wash and dry lettuce (make sure it is very dry), and rip into bite-size pieces.

Place in large salad bowl. Toss in Parmesan cheese.

Place Camembert and goat cheeses on a nonstick cookie sheet to melt in oven for 1 minute.

Place cheese wedges on salad. Top with dressing and serve.

TOTAL GRAMS 33.5
GRAMS PER SERVING 4.2

Salad Dressings

Mustard Vinaigrette

20 tablespoons

1 teaspoon Dijon mustard
¼ teaspoon dry mustard
2 tablespoons fresh dill, minced
1 tablespoon balsamic vinegar
½ teaspoon seasoned salt
1 cup extra-virgin olive oil

Beat ingredients together in a small bowl until well blended. Refrigerate for ½ hour.

TOTAL GRAMS   4.6
GRAMS PER SERVING   0.2

Lime Dill Dressing (vinegar-free)

18 tablespoons

1 cup extra-virgin olive oil
1 teaspoon Dijon mustard
¼ teaspoon dry mustard
juice of 1 lime
¼ teaspoon seasoned salt
1 clove garlic, minced
1 tablespoon dill, minced
pinch sugar substitute

Beat ingredients together in a small bowl. Refrigerate for ½ hour.

TOTAL GRAMS   3.7
GRAMS PER SERVING   0.2

Tomato Mayonnaise (without vinegar)

20 tablespoons

1 organic egg
1 teaspoon lemon juice
½ teaspoon seasoned salt
¼ teaspoon dried mustard
¾ cup olive oil
1 small ripe tomato, peeled and seeded
2 tablespoon fresh basil, minced

Place first 4 ingredients in a food processor and blend. Add oil in a slow steady stream until it is fully blended. Chop tomato pulp and add to food processor with the basil. Blend for 30 seconds.

TOTAL GRAMS 9.0
GRAMS PER TABLESPOON 0.5

Basic Vinegar-Free Salad Dressing

16 tablespoons

1 teaspoon seasoned salt
¼ teaspoon black pepper
1 teaspoon dry mustard
dash of Tabasco sauce
¼ lemon juice
⅔ cup olive oil

Beat all ingredients together. Refrigerate.

TOTAL GRAMS 1.0
GRAMS PER SERVING 0.6

Vinegar-Free Mayonnaise

20 tablespoons

1 organic egg
2 tablespoons lemon juice
1 teaspoon Dijon mustard
¼ teaspoon dry mustard
¼ teaspoon seasoned salt
1 cup olive oil

Place first 5 ingredients in blender. Drizzle oil into blender very slowly in a steady stream until it is fully blended.

TOTAL GRAMS   4.6
GRAMS PER TABLESPOON   0.2

Vinegar-Free Mustard

2 tablespoon (1 serving)

2 tablespoons Vinegar-Free Mayonnaise
¼ teaspoon dry mustard

Blend well. For more of a mustard flavor, increase dry mustard.

TOTAL GRAMS   0.5

Our Favorite Roquefort Dressing

16 tablespoons

¼ cup tarragon vinegar
¼ teaspoon seasoned salt
3 turns of pepper mill
6 tablespoons olive oil
2 tablespoons heavy cream
½ teaspoon lemon juice
¼ cup crumbled Roquefort cheese

Beat all ingredients together except cheese. Stir in cheese.

TOTAL GRAMS   6.7
GRAMS PER TABLESPOON   0.4

Basic French Dressing

12 tablespoons

3 tablespoons tarragon vinegar
1 tablespoon lemon juice
½ teaspoon seasoned salt
3 turns of pepper mill
6 tablespoons olive oil
2 tablespoons vegetable oil
½ teaspoon Dijon mustard
¼ teaspoon dry mustard

Beat all ingredients together until well blended.

TOTAL GRAMS   2.5
GRAMS PER TABLESPOON   0.2

Vinaigrette Cream Dressing

32 tablespoons

½ cup tarragon vinegar
¾ teaspoon salt
¼ teaspoon cracked pepper
1½ cups olive oil (or ½ cup olive oil and 1 cup vegetable oil)
1 teaspoon chopped green olives
1 teaspoon chopped parsley
3 tablespoons sour cream
1 yolk from hard-boiled egg, finely chopped

Mix vinegar, salt, and pepper. Add oil, olives, parsley, sour cream, and chopped yolk.

Beat well with fork. Chill for several hours.

TOTAL GRAMS 8.2
GRAMS PER TABLESPOON 0.3

Dressing of the House

10 tablespoons

2 tablespoons olive oil
4 tablespoons vegetable oil
2 tablespoons tarragon vinegar
1 teaspoon seasoned salt
1 teaspoon Dijon mustard
¼ teaspoon garlic
1 tablespoon mayonnaise
¼ teaspoon sugar substitute

Put all ingredients in screw-top jar. Close jar and shake until everything is well blended. Refrigerate.

TOTAL GRAMS 3.5
GRAMS PER TABLESPOON 0.4

Thousand Island Dressing

20 tablespoons

6 scallions
1 kosher dill pickle
2 tomatoes
½ teaspoon garlic powder
1 teaspoon seasoned salt
2 tablespoons olive oil
2 tablespoons tarragon vinegar
2 tablespoons mayonnaise

Chop scallions, pickle, and tomatoes together in wooden chopping bowl. Add rest of ingredients and mix well. Refrigerate.

TOTAL GRAMS   22.1
GRAMS PER SERVING   1.1

Creamy Celery Seed Dressing

19 tablespoons

½ cup sour cream
½ cup mayonnaise
2 tablespoons tomato sauce
½ teaspoon Worcestershire sauce
½ teaspoon celery seed
½ teaspoon seasoned salt

Combine all ingredients in a screw-top jar. Shake well. Refrigerate.

TOTAL GRAMS   9.8
GRAMS PER TABLESPOON   0.5

Dill Vinaigrette Dressing

16 tablespoons

4 tablespoons tarragon vinegar
2 tablespoons olive oil
6 tablespoons safflower oil
2 tablespoons chopped olives
¼ teaspoon dry mustard
1 teaspoon Dijon mustard
1 teaspoon lemon juice
¼ teaspoon garlic powder
2 teaspoons dry dill (or 2 tablespoons fresh dill)
½ packet sugar substitute
1 organic egg

Place all ingredients in a screw-top jar. Shake well. Refrigerate.

TOTAL GRAMS 4.4
GRAMS PER TABLESPOON 0.3

Curry Dressing

14 tablespoons

4 tablespoons tarragon vinegar
2 tablespoons olive oil
6 tablespoons safflower oil
1 teaspoon lemon juice
½ teaspoon curry
1 tablespoon sour cream
¼ teaspoon garlic powder
1 teaspoon sesame seeds
½ teaspoon seasoned salt
1 organic egg

Place all ingredients in a screw-top jar. Shake well. Refrigerate.

TOTAL GRAMS 5.3
GRAMS PER SERVING 0.4

Italian Dressing

14 tablespoons

½ cup olive oil
¼ cup wine vinegar
1 clove garlic, minced
½ teaspoon seasoned salt
¼ teaspoon pepper

Combine all ingredients in a screw-top jar. Shake well. Refrigerate. Shake again before serving.

TOTAL GRAMS 3.3
GRAMS PER SERVING 0.2

Parmesan Caesar Dressing

14 tablespoons

4 tablespoons tarragon vinegar
2 tablespoons olive oil
6 tablespoons safflower oil
1 teaspoon lemon juice
¼ teaspoon dry mustard
2 teaspoons Dijon mustard
1 teaspoon grated Parmesan cheese
¼ teaspoon garlic powder
1 teaspoon seasoned salt
½ packet sugar substitute
1 organic egg

Place all ingredients in a screw-top jar. Shake well. Refrigerate.

TOTAL GRAMS 4.6
GRAMS PER TABLESPOON 0.3

Meat

Oriental Beef Stir Fry

4 servings

½ pound spinach, steamed and drained
1½ pounds beef tenderloin
6 tablespoons sesame oil
4 tablespoons Tamari soy sauce
pepper to taste
½ pound shiitake mushrooms, sliced
1 onion, sliced thin
4 ounces bamboo shoots, cut into thin strips
3 stalks celery, cut into thin strips
2 tablespoons sake
½ cup Beef Stock

Drain spinach well. Cut meat into thin strips and sauté in a large skillet using half of the hot sesame oil. Brown meat on both sides. Sprinkle with 2 tablespoons soy sauce and pepper. Remove meat from skillet. Put mushrooms, onions, bamboo shoots, and celery into skillet. Sauté for 3 minutes. Return beef to pan, add spinach and toss with soy sauce, sake, and stock. Cook over low heat for 6–8 minutes or to desired doneness.

TOTAL GRAMS 27.0
GRAMS PER SERVING 6.8

Kayzie's Rabbit

6 servings

1 3–4 pound frying rabbit
½ cup olive oil plus olive oil for sautéeing
juice of 1 large lemon
½ teaspoon rosemary
½ teaspoon fennel seeds
½ teaspoon seasoned salt
8 cloves of garlic, minced
1 large onion, sliced thin
4 small carrots, sliced thin
2 bay leaves
¼ pound thick-sliced bacon
1 cup shiitake mushrooms, sliced
2 cups Chicken Stock

Wash and dry rabbit.

Mix ½ cup olive oil, lemon juice, rosemary, fennel, salt, and garlic in a large bowl. Add onions and carrots.

Spread ½ of vegetable mixture on bottom of a roasting pan. Place rabbit pieces on top. Top with remaining vegetable mixture. Place bay leaves on top. Cover bowl and place in refrigerator for 2 days. Sprinkle with olive oil daily.

To cook:

Remove rabbit from vegetable mixture, and save the vegetables.

Slice bacon into bite-size pieces and brown in a large skillet. Add ½ cup olive oil to skillet and brown rabbit pieces well on all sides. Remove and set aside.

Strain vegetable mixture to get rid of excess liquid. Place vegetables and mushrooms in hot skillet and lightly brown. Remove vegetables with a slotted spoon and empty oil from pan. Place vegetables and rabbit back into pan, cover with *Chicken Stock,* heat to a simmer cover and cook for 1½ hours.

TOTAL GRAMS **78.6**
GRAMS PER SERVING **13.1**

Mother's Pot Roast

6 servings

3½ pound rump roast
garlic powder
seasoned salt
2 medium onions, sliced
3 tomatoes, skinned
2 cloves of garlic

Rub garlic powder and seasoned salt into the meat. Place in refrigerator for ½ hour.

Place onions and garlic in a food processor. Push tomatoes through a strainer to rid them of seeds and place tomato pulp in food processor. Puree.

Place meat in a large pot. Cover with tomato sauce and simmer for 1½ hours. Turn meat and simmer about 1½ hours more or until fork-soft. Remove meat from pot to a wooden cutting board to cool. Place sauce in refrigerator to allow fat to rise to top. When meat is cool, slice. Remove fat that has formed on the sauce and place meat back in the sauce. Warm and serve.

TOTAL GRAMS 27.3
GRAMS PER SERVING 4.6

THE HAMBURGERS

Dr. Atkins' Fromage Burger

6 servings

2 pounds beef, ground
1 tablespoon chives, chopped
¾ teaspoon tarragon, crumbled
2 teaspoons seasoned salt
¼ cup fresh parsley, chopped
¼ cup scallions, minced
1 small tomato, diced
1 egg, beaten
6 ounces Cheddar cheese, coarsely grated
3 tablespoons butter, melted (optional)

Combine beef, chives, tarragon, salt, parsley, scallions, tomato, and egg. Mix well.

Shape into 12 equal balls. Flatten each ball to pancake shape. Divide cheese into 6 piles. Press cheese together. Place 1 pile of cheese in the center of 6 of the meat pancakes. Place second meat pancake on top. Press edges together to seal.

Dr. Atkins likes to cook these on an outdoor grill. If one is not available, broil in oven or sauté with butter in a nonstick skillet for five minutes on each side.

TOTAL GRAMS   19.5
GRAMS PER SERVING   3.5

Brit Burgers

2 servings

4 tablespoons butter
½ cup onions, chopped
1 pound beef, ground
½ teaspoon seasoned salt

½ teaspoon pepper
½ teaspoon sage

Melt 2 tablespoons butter in a skillet. Sauté onions until golden. Remove and set aside.

In same skillet, melt remaining 2 tablespoons butter. Add beef, salt, pepper, and sage to onions and mix well. Shape into patties. Broil in oven or sauté for 5 minutes on each side.

TOTAL GRAMS   8.8
GRAMS PER SERVING   4.4

Pizza Burgers

6 servings

2 pounds beef, ground
1 teaspoon seasoned salt
1 tablespoon parsley, chopped
⅛ teaspoon basil
⅛ teaspoon oregano
2 eggs, beaten
1 package fried pork rinds, crushed
¼ cup olive oil
6 slices mozzarella cheese
½ recipe Pasta Sauce
3 tablespoons grated Parmesan cheese

Preheat oven to 400° F.

Mix beef with salt, parsley, basil, and oregano.

Shape into 6 patties ½-inch thick.

Dip patties into eggs, then coat with crushed pork rinds. Sauté patties in hot olive oil until well browned on both sides. Arrange in a shallow baking dish. They must not be touching. Top each patty with a slice of mozzarella cheese. Pour on *Pasta Sauce*. Sprinkle with Parmesan cheese. Bake for 15 minutes. If cheese is not bubbly, place under broiler for 1 minute.

TOTAL GRAMS   46.2
GRAMS PER SERVING   7.7

Feta Burgers

2 servings

2 tablespoons butter
1 pound beef, ground
¼ cup crumbled feta cheese
¼ cup finely chopped black olives
½ teaspoon seasoned salt
½ teaspoon pepper

Melt butter in a heavy skillet.
  Mix remaining ingredients, and shape into patties.
  Sauté hamburgers for 5 minutes on each side.

TOTAL GRAMS 7.4
GRAMS PER SERVING 3.7

Curry Burgers

2 servings

2 tablespoons butter
1 pound beef, ground
1 tablespoon finely chopped walnuts
2 teaspoons curry powder
½ teaspoon seasoned salt

Melt butter in a skillet.
  Mix remainder of ingredients and shape into patties.
  Sauté hamburgers for 5 minutes on each side.

TOTAL GRAMS 5.4
GRAMS PER SERVING 2.7

¡Ole! Burgers

2 servings

2 tablespoons butter
1 pound beef, ground
6 drops Tabasco sauce
½ teaspoon cumin
½ teaspoon chili powder
¼ teaspoon garlic powder

Melt butter in a skillet.
  Mix remainder of ingredients and shape into patties.
  Sauté hamburgers for 5 minutes on each side.

TOTAL GRAMS 0.8
GRAMS PER SERVING 0.4

U.S. Hamburgers

2 servings

6 strips lean bacon
1 ripe tomato, finely chopped
2 tablespoons butter
1 pound beef, ground
½ teaspoon seasoned salt
½ teaspoon pepper

Fry bacon until crisp. Remove from pan, and place on paper towels to drain and crisp. Crumble bacon into a large bowl. Sauté tomato in bacon fat until tender. Add it to the bacon. Pour off bacon fat and melt butter in same skillet. Combine meat, salt, and pepper with bacon and tomato.
  Shape into patties.
  Sauté hamburgers for 5 minutes on each side.

TOTAL GRAMS 6.2
GRAMS PER SERVING 3.1

Steak Au Poivre

4 servings

4 shell steaks, pounded to ⅛-inch thickness
freshly ground black pepper
6 tablespoons butter
2 teaspoons rosemary
2 teaspoons sage
4 ounces cognac, warmed
6 ounces heavy cream
2 teaspoons Worcestershire sauce
2 tablespoons Dijon mustard

Cover surface of steaks on both sides with ground pepper.

Press pepper into steaks.

In a large skillet melt butter and add rosemary and sage.

Add steaks and brown quickly on both sides. Ignite warm cognac and pour over steaks. When fire goes out, remove steaks from skillet and keep warm.

Add cream, Worcestershire, and mustard to pan juices. Stir well and simmer for 3 minutes. Pour over steak and serve.

TOTAL GRAMS   9.2
GRAMS PER SERVING   4.6

Moussaka

6 servings

1 medium eggplant
1 pound ground lamb or ½-pound ground chuck
8 teaspoons sweet butter
3 egg yolks
1¼ cups water
¼ cup heavy cream
½ cup grated Parmesan cheese
6 tablespoons olive oil
1 large onion, chopped

1 large green pepper, chopped
2 cloves garlic, minced
1 8-ounce can tomato sauce
1½ teaspoons cumin
¼ teaspoon nutmeg
½ teaspoon oregano
2 teaspoons salt

Preheat oven to 350° F.

To prepare cream sauce:
Place butter in top of double boiler over hot water. Add egg yolks one at a time. Beat constantly with rotary or hand electric beater. Add ¼ cup water, cream, and Parmesan cheese. Continue to beat until sauce thickens, about 10 minutes.

Pare and slice eggplant. Sprinkle salt on slices. Arrange eggplant on a large plate. Place plate in sink. Cover with another large plate, allowing plate to press eggplant. Let drain for ½ hour, then press each slice with a paper towel. Heat 2 tablespoons olive oil in a large skillet. Add onion and green pepper. Sauté until light brown. Add garlic and meat.

Add tomato sauce, 1 cup water, cumin, nutmeg, oregano, and salt. Simmer for 15 minutes.

Heat remaining 4 tablespoons of olive oil, and sauté eggplant slices until lightly brown. Drain on paper towels. Place half the eggplant slices in a well-oiled baking dish. Spread with half the meat mixture. Place remaining eggplant slices on top and cover with the rest of the meat. Cover top with cream sauce.

Bake for 30 minutes.

TOTAL GRAMS 39.6
GRAMS PER SERVING 6.6

Calves Liver in Red Wine

4 servings

6 shallots or 1 small onion, finely chopped
1 cup dry red wine
juice of 1 lemon
4 tablespoons oil
½ teaspoon oregano
½ teaspoon seasoned salt
¼ teaspoon black pepper
1 pound calves liver, sliced
4 tablespoons butter

Combine shallots, wine, lemon juice, oil, oregano, salt, and pepper in a large bowl. Marinate liver for 1 hour, then turn it and marinate for another hour.

Remove liver from marinade.

Melt butter in a skillet, and sauté liver for 5 minutes on each side.

TOTAL GRAMS 7.2
GRAMS PER SERVING 1.8

Veal Rolatine

4 servings

4 veal cutlets, flattened with a mallet
½ teaspoon seasoned salt
4 slices prosciutto ham
6 slices Jarlsberg cheese
1 egg, beaten
¼ cup grated Parmesan cheese
4 tablespoons sweet butter
¼ cup dry white wine

Preheat oven to 350° F.

Wash and dry veal. Sprinkle with salt. Place 1 slice of ham and 1 slice of cheese on each cutlet. Roll up and tie with string. Dip rolls in egg and coat with Parmesan cheese. Place in refrigerator for ½ hour to set. Melt butter in a heavy skillet. Sauté veal rolls until they are brown on all sides. Remove rolls to a small baking dish. Add wine to pan juices and bring to a boil. Pour sauce over rolls. Top with 2 remaining slices of cheese. Bake for ½ hour. Remove string and serve.

Note: This may be used as an hors d'oeuvre by cutting rolls into pieces the size of half dollars.

TOTAL GRAMS 4.0
GRAMS PER SERVING 1.0

Gourmet Pork Chops

6 servings

12 pork chops
salt and pepper to taste
2 tablespoons garlic oil
2 tablespoons olive oil
1 onion, chopped
1 clove garlic, minced
1 pound mushrooms, sliced
1½ cups hot Chicken Stock
½ cup dry red wine
1 bay leaf
¼ cup sour cream (optional)

Preheat oven to 350° F.

Sprinkle pork chops with salt and pepper. In a heavy skillet brown chops in garlic oil over high heat. Remove and keep warm. Add olive oil to pan. Sauté onion, garlic, and mushrooms in olive oil until onion is golden. Pour in *Chicken Stock,* wine, and add bay leaf. Bring mixture to a boil and cook for about 3 minutes.

Arrange 6 pork chops in casserole. Top with half the vegetables from mixture (remove them with slotted spoon).

Put another layer of pork chops on top and pour over remaining mixture. Cover casserole tightly and bake for 1½ hours.

If desired, sour cream may be added to mixture when served.

TOTAL GRAMS   36.9
GRAMS PER SERVING   6.2

Roast Veal

6 servings

1 4–5 pounds veal roast (leg, loin, rump, shoulder, or breast)
1 clove garlic, minced
½ pound thick-sliced bacon
3 tablespoons olive oil
4 tablespoons chopped onion
2 celery stalks, diced
4 anchovies (optional)
½ cup white wine or Chicken Stock

Preheat oven to 325° F.

Have the butcher bone and tie meat. Cut a few incisions in veal and insert minced garlic.

In roasting pan with cover, heat oil and brown veal. Add onion, celery, and wine (or stock) to pan. Arrange bacon on top. Place in oven. Cover and baste occasionally. Cook for 30 minutes to the pound. Remove veal from pan, and let it set for 10 minutes for easier carving. Remove vegetables from pan juices, skim off excess fat, and pour pan juices over veal. Serve warm, or serve cold-sliced with *Vinaigrette Cream Dressing*.

TOTAL GRAMS   16.0
GRAMS PER SERVING   2.4

Veal Scallopini at Its Best

6 servings

1½ pounds veal cut into scallops ¼-inch thick
salt and pepper to taste
6 tablespoons butter
¼ cup brandy
1 cup Chicken Stock
¼ cup Chablis
2 tablespoons dry sherry
1 pound porcini mushrooms, sliced
2 tomatoes, peeled
1 teaspoon garlic powder
½ cup grated Swiss cheese
¼ cup grated Parmesan cheese

Preheat broiler.

Pat salt and pepper into veal.

In a skillet melt butter, then add veal to brown.

Heat brandy. Ignite it. Pour over veal. Remove veal from skillet and keep warm. Pour *Chicken Stock,* Chablis, and sherry in skillet. Simmer until liquid reduces to half. Return veal to skillet. Simmer for 10 minutes. Keep warm until serving.

Sauté mushrooms in 2 tablespoons butter until brown. Add peeled tomatoes and garlic powder. Simmer for 5 minutes. Place mushroom mixture in baking dish. Add veal and cover with wine sauce. Sprinkle with grated Swiss and Parmesan cheeses.

Broil until cheese is brown and bubbly. Serve immediately.

TOTAL GRAMS 40.5
GRAMS PER SERVING 6.7

My Grandmother's Veal Stew

4 servings

3 strips bacon, diced
3 tablespoons butter
1 tablespoon chopped onion
½ cup sliced mushrooms
2 pounds cubed veal
½ cup water or Chicken Stock
1 cup sour cream
1 teaspoon salt
¼ teaspoon paprika

Preheat oven to 250° F.

Place bacon, butter, onion, and mushrooms in skillet. Sauté slowly until onion and bacon are lightly brown. Remove mixture with slotted spoon. Place in ovenproof baking dish. Leave bacon fat and butter in skillet, then add veal. Brown meat on all sides. Remove veal, leaving fat in skillet. Place meat in baking dish. Mix well with bacon mixture.

Add water (or stock), sour cream, salt, and paprika to fat in skillet. Heat just to boiling. Pour over meat mixture. Cover dish. Bake for 1 hour, or until veal is tender when pierced with fork.

TOTAL GRAMS   17.4
GRAMS PER SERVING   4.3

Garden Beef

8 servings

4 tablespoons vegetable oil
3 pounds stew meat (chuck, round)
4 tablespoons onion, chopped
4 cups water
3 soup bones
2 teaspoons salt
½ cup cubed rutabaga
½ cup cubed zucchini
4 tablespoons tomato sauce
1 cup spinach

Heat oil in large heavy pot. Add meat and brown well on all sides. Push meat to one side of pot, and add onion. Cook 2 more minutes.

Add water, soup bones, and salt. Simmer for 2 hours.

Add rutabaga and simmer for 15 more minutes.

Add green pepper, eggplant, and zucchini. Simmer for 10 more minutes. Spoon in tomato sauce and spinach, and cook for 7 more minutes.

TOTAL GRAMS 43.9
GRAMS PER SERVING 5.4

Luscious Lamb

4 servings

8 lamb chops
garlic powder
2 tablespoons butter
2 tablespoons Worcestershire sauce
2 tablespoons lemon juice
2 tablespoons gin
1 teaspoon seasoned salt

Rub lamb chops with small amount of garlic powder. Melt butter and add Worcestershire sauce, lemon juice, gin, and salt in a small pan. Pour liquid over lamb chops. Allow to marinate in refrigerator for 30 minutes. Remove lamb from marinade. Broil or barbecue to desired doneness. Top with marinade before serving.

TOTAL GRAMS   2.8
GRAMS PER SERVING   0.7

Stuffed Leg of Lamb

8 servings

2 tablespoons butter
1 pound veal or beef, ground
3 tablespoons chopped onion
1 clove garlic, minced
½ cup white wine
1 8-ounce can tomato sauce
1 tablespoon dill
1 tablespoon chopped parsley
½ cup grated Parmesan cheese
salt and pepper to taste
1 leg of lamb, boned and flattened

Preheat oven to 300° F.

Melt 1 tablespoon butter in heavy skillet. Add ground meat, onion, and garlic. Brown lightly on all sides. Pour wine in pan slowly, and cook for 2 minutes. Add tomato sauce, dill, and parsley. Cook over medium heat for 10 minutes or until liquid has been absorbed. Remove from heat. Pour off fat. Sprinkle with Parmesan cheese, salt, and pepper. Wipe lamb with damp cloth. Sprinkle with salt and pepper.

Spread ground meat mixture on lamb and roll up carefully. Use skewers to fasten it or tie with string.

Melt 1 tablespoon butter in medium-size roasting pan. Add lamb roll. Brown over medium heat.

Bake for 2 hours or until meat is tender. (If the pan gets dry, add 2 or 3 tablespoons water to pan.)

TOTAL GRAMS 29.5
GRAMS PER SERVING 3.5

Loin of Lamb with Horseradish Cream

6 servings

2 3-pound lamb loins (boned and trimmed of fat), use bones for stock
3 bay leaves
3 ribs of celery, quartered
6 black peppercorns
1 clove garlic, quartered
1 onion, chopped
¼ cup walnut oil
salt and freshly ground pepper to taste
2 cups heavy cream
3 tablespoons white horseradish, drained
2 tablespoons snipped chives

Place lamb bones, bay leaf, celery, and peppercorns in 4 cups of water. Bring water to a boil, skimming broth, and simmer mixture until liquid is reduced to about 2½ cups. Strain stock through a fine sieve into a pan. Add garlic and onions. Bring liquid to a boil. Simmer until it is reduced to 1½ cups. Strain the stock.

In a large skillet, heat oil over medium heat until it is hot (do not allow it to smoke). Season lamb with salt and pepper and brown in oil. Turn lamb to brown well on all sides. Remove lamb from oil, cool for 10 minutes, and slice it into ½-inch-thick slices. Arrange it on a platter and keep it warm. Return stock to skillet, and stir in cream and horseradish. Gently simmer sauce until it thickens (do not boil). Adjust seasonings and spoon over lamb.

TOTAL GRAMS 32.4
GRAMS PER SERVING 5.4

Steak Pizzaiola

6 servings

⅛ cup garlic oil
¼ cup olive oil
2 tablespoons tarragon vinegar
1 teaspoon water
freshly cracked black pepper
3 pounds sirloin steak
8 Italian plum tomatoes, cut into strips (1 cup)
2 cloves garlic, crushed
1 tablespoon chopped parsley
1 teaspoon oregano
⅛ teaspoon seasoned salt
4 tablespoons pine nuts
½ packet sugar substitute

Combine garlic oil with ⅛ cup olive oil, vinegar, water, and pepper. Place steak in mixture and marinate in refrigerator for at least 2 hours, preferably overnight. Heat remaining olive oil, and add tomatoes, garlic, parsley, oregano, salt, and pine nuts. Cook over medium heat for 3 minutes. Remove from heat, add sugar substitute, and keep warm. Broil steak to desired doneness, slice, and pour mixture over it. Serve immediately.

TOTAL GRAMS 17.6
GRAMS PER SERVING 2.9

Cabbage Rolls Stuffed with Meat (Dolma)

6 servings

1 medium cabbage
1½ pound lamb or beef, ground
4 tablespoons diced onion
4 tablespoons chopped parsley
2 eggs
1 teaspoon salt
pepper to taste
⅓ cup tomato sauce

Sauce:
1 cup chopped cabbage
½ cup water
⅔ can tomato sauce (8 ounces)
2 tablespoons lemon juice
2 packets sugar substitute

Clean cabbage and remove any damaged leaves. Pour boiling water over cabbage. Cover and let stand for ½ hour. Mix ground meat, onion, parsley, eggs, salt, pepper, and tomato sauce together.

Drain cabbage, core, and separate leaves.

To stuff:
Use 12 leaves. Put 2 full tablespoons of meat mixture in center of each leaf. Bring sides up over filling and roll leaf up. Set aside.

Sauce:
Chop remaining cabbage (the core and leaves not suitable for stuffing). Heat water in a medium-size pot. Bring to boil. Add chopped cabbage, tomato sauce, salt, lemon juice, and sugar substitute. Turn heat down. Cover and simmer for 15 minutes.

Remove 1 cup sauce and set aside. Place cabbage rolls in pot with remaining sauce as close together as possible. Pour cup of sauce over cabbage rolls. Cover. Simmer for 1½ hours.

TOTAL GRAMS   50.8
GRAMS PER SERVING   8.3

Spicy Spareribs

4 servings

4 pounds pork spareribs (or beef ribs)
1 tablespoon paprika
2 teaspoons chili powder
¾ teaspoon salt
¼ teaspoon dry mustard
¼ teaspoon garlic powder
⅛ teaspoon pepper

Preheat oven to 450° F.

Place single layer of ribs, meaty side down, in shallow roasting pan. Roast for ½ hour. Drain off fat. Combine rest of ingredients. Place in saltshaker. Sprinkle evenly over ribs.

Reduce oven to 350° F. Roast, meaty side up, for spareribs, ½–1 hour longer. (Beef ribs will take about 1 hour longer.)

TOTAL GRAMS   TRACE
GRAMS PER SERVING   0.0

Stuffed Steak

6 servings

garlic powder
3 pounds of any cut of steak (cut with pockets)
½ pound shiitake mushrooms
½ teaspoon thyme
3 sprigs parsley (tops only)
5 slices smoked ham
2 tablespoons sweet butter
2 shallots or 1 small onion, finely chopped
1 clove garlic, chopped
2 tablespoons dry white wine

Rub garlic powder on steak and set aside.

Chop together mushrooms, thyme, parsley, and ham in large wooden chopping bowl.

Heat butter over low flame until melted and bubbles disappear. Brown shallots and garlic in butter. Add mushroom mixture and cook for 3 minutes, stirring occasionally. Add wine and cook 1 more minute. Remove from heat and spoon mushroom mixture into pockets in steak. Stuff firmly, and sew closed with a trussing needle and thread.

Broil steak to desired doneness.

Serve with hot *Parsley Butter Sauce.*

TOTAL GRAMS   18.6
GRAMS PER SERVING   3.1

Pork Loin with Mustard

6 servings

6 ½-inch slices of boneless pork loin
salt and freshly ground black pepper
2 tablespoons olive oil
2 tablespoons onion, minced
¼ cup dry white wine
2 teaspoons brandy
¾ cup Chicken Stock
2 packets sugar substitute
1 tablespoon Dijon mustard

Season pork well with salt and pepper.

Heat oil in a large skillet over medium heat. Do not allow it to smoke. Brown pork in oil. Remove pork, lower heat, and add shallots. Cook them for about 3 minutes. Pour in wine and brandy and simmer until liquid has evaporated. Add stock and sugar substitute. Whisk mixture as it boils until liquid is reduced by half. Add pork and simmer for about 2 minutes until pork is warm and has absorbed sauce. Remove pork to a serving plate. Whisk mustard into sauce, correct seasonings and spoon sauce over pork.

TOTAL GRAMS   5.1
GRAMS PER SERVING   0.8

Poultry

Chicken Cacciatore

8 servings

1 5-pound chicken, cut into 8 pieces
½ cup olive oil
4 tablespoons butter
⅓ cup chopped onion
½ pound shiitake mushrooms, sliced
3 cloves garlic
¾ cup dry white wine
2 bay leaves
1 teaspoon basil
½ teaspoon freshly ground black pepper
5 tablespoons tomato sauce
seasoned salt to taste
2 tablespoons brandy

Sauté chicken in olive oil until light brown.

Heat butter in skillet. When it stops bubbling, add onion and mushrooms and sauté until golden. Add garlic. Cook for 4 more minutes. Spoon mushrooms, onions, and garlic over chicken. Pour on wine. Add bay leaves, basil, and pepper. Simmer for about 8 minutes, uncovered. Stir in tomato sauce. Salt to taste. Cook, uncovered, for 2 more minutes. Add brandy, and serve.

TOTAL GRAMS 24.5
GRAMS PER SERVING 3.0

Lemon-Basted Roast Chicken

4 servings

1 chicken, cut up
½ teaspoon oregano
¼ teaspoon garlic powder
¼ cup butter (½ stick)
salt and pepper to taste
juice of 2 lemons (6 to 8 tablespoons)

Preheat oven to 400° F.

Sprinkle chicken with oregano and garlic powder. Melt butter in roasting pan or casserole. Roll chicken in it. Sprinkle with salt and pepper.

Roast chicken skin side up, uncovered, for 30 minutes or until golden brown. Turn pieces over and continue roasting until brown (about 30 more minutes). Reduce heat to 300° F. and cook until tender. Squeeze lemon juice over chicken.

Cover and let sit in turned-off oven for 15 minutes.

Remove to platter and serve.

TOTAL GRAMS 9.3
GRAMS PER SERVING 2.3

Coq Au Vin with Shiitake Mushrooms

8 servings

4 slices thick-sliced bacon
7 tablespoons butter
4 pounds chicken, cut up
1 teaspoon seasoned salt
¼ cup cognac (or brandy)
1 cup dry red wine
1 cup Chicken Stock
¼ teaspoon garlic powder
¾ teaspoon thyme
1 bay leaf
4 medium-size onions, sliced
½ pound shiitake mushrooms, sliced
chopped chives

Dice bacon and sauté in 4 tablespoons butter in large skillet until brown. Remove bacon from skillet and save.

Wash and thoroughly dry chicken. Brown in bacon fat and season.

Put bacon back in pan, cover, and simmer for about 10 minutes. Heat cognac in small pan. Ignite, and pour over chicken. Add wine, stock, garlic powder, and thyme. Bury bay leaf in chicken, cover and simmer for 45 minutes. Remove chicken and keep warm.

Boil liquid in pan until it reduces by half.

Sauté onions and mushrooms in 3 tablespoons butter until onions are golden.

Put chicken back into skillet with mushrooms and onions around it. Simmer for 5 minutes. Garnish with chives.

TOTAL GRAMS 58.5
GRAMS PER SERVING 7.4

Chicken à la Firenze

4 servings

4 boneless chicken breasts
2 eggs, beaten
½ package fried pork rinds, crushed
3 tablespoons butter
½ cup Sautérne
1 cup Chicken Stock
1 clove garlic, crushed
dash of marjaram
dash of basil
⅓ cup cream
½ pound spinach, cooked*
¼ cup grated Parmesan cheese

Preheat oven to 350° F.

Dip chicken in eggs and dredge in crushed pork rinds until well coated. Sauté in butter until chicken begins to brown. Turn once. Lower heat. Add wine and cook until wine has almost evaporated.

Remove from heat.

Mix together stock, garlic, marjoram, basil, and cream to make a sauce.

Place ½ spinach in bottom of casserole. Add chicken and rest of spinach. Pour sauce over top. Sprinkle with Parmesan cheese and bake for ½ hour.

TOTAL GRAMS 18.5
GRAMS PER SERVING 4.6

*To cook fresh spinach: Wash carefully several times to remove all sand. Place in pot with just enough water to cover it. Cook at low boil for about 20 minutes or until tender, but not limp. Press out water before serving. Two packages of frozen spinach may be substituted for fresh spinach. Cook to package directions. Whether fresh or frozen do not overcook.

Summer Day Chicken From Spain

4 servings

1 5-pound chicken, or chicken pieces
¼ cup safflower oil
2 cloves garlic
juice of 1 lemon
1 teaspoon grated orange rind
2 bay leaves
½ cup vinegar
1 cup white wine
1 cup Chicken Stock
½ teaspoon coarsely ground pepper
salt to taste

Wash and dry chicken. Heat oil in skillet. Lightly brown chicken over medium heat.

Combine remaining ingredients for marinade. Pour over chicken. Simmer, covered, for 1 hour. Add more stock, if necessary, to keep chicken covered.

When chicken is done, place in refrigerator, covered with marinade.

Serve cold in marinade.

TOTAL GRAMS 23.3
GRAMS PER SERVING 6.0

Austrian Paprika Chicken

6 servings

2 tablespoons butter
2 tablespoons vegetable oil
2 chicken broilers, cut up
seasoned salt
4 small onions
1 clove garlic, minced
2 tablespoons paprika
1 cup Chicken Stock
1 cup sour cream

Preheat oven to 350° F.

Heat butter and oil together. Brown chicken carefully in oil on all sides. Add salt. Remove chicken from pan.

Place onions and garlic in oil and sauté until onions are golden. Add paprika, stock, and sour cream. Stir constantly until mixture is smooth.

Place chicken in casserole and cover with mixture, making sure to scrape pan well of all drippings.

Bake, covered, for 1 hour.

Serve with *Tossed Salad with Tomato Dressing*.

TOTAL GRAMS 21.7
GRAMS PER SERVING 4.6

Chicken Croquettes

2 servings

1½ cups chicken, ground
2 egg whites
¼ teaspoon poultry seasoning
pinch of salt
walnut oil for deep frying
2 tablespoons chopped onion
4 large mushrooms, chopped
1 tablespoon butter
Cream Sauce

Preheat oven to 375° F.

Mix chicken, egg whites, poultry seasoning, and salt. Form into croquettes 1-inch wide and 3-inches long. Fry in deep fat until crisp.

Sauté mushrooms and onion in oil until lightly browned.

Prepare *Cream Sauce.*

Place mushrooms and onions in a casserole and arrange croquettes on top.

Pour sauce on top.

Bake for about 8–10 minutes until thoroughly heated.

To make a prettier dish, place sliced hard-boiled eggs between croquettes. Then add sauce. Sprinkle with paprika.

TOTAL GRAMS   5.3
GRAMS PER SERVING   3.0

Gourmet Game Hens

6 servings

¾ cup butter
¾ cup white port wine
3 tablespoons dried tarragon
6 garlic cloves
1½ teaspoons salt
¾ teaspoon pepper

6 frozen Rock Cornish hens, about 1¼ pounds each, thawed
garlic powder

Preheat oven to 400° F.

Melt butter in a saucepan. Add wine and 1 tablespoon dried tarragon.

Place 1 garlic clove, 1 teaspoon tarragon, ¼ teaspoon salt, and ⅛ teaspoon pepper in each hen. Sprinkle outside liberally with garlic powder.

Pour wine sauce over hens and roast in large shallow pan, without rack, for about 1 hour or until well browned and drumstick twists easily. Baste frequently with sauce.

TOTAL GRAMS   9.2
GRAMS PER SERVING   1.4

Turkey à la King

4 servings

4 egg yolks
¼ teaspoon seasoned salt
½ teaspoon dry tarragon
1 cup heavy cream
1 cup Chicken Stock
2 cups diced turkey meat
nutmeg

Preheat oven to 350° F.

Beat yolks until thick and lemon-colored. Add salt and tarragon. Beat in heavy cream. Stir in stock, then add turkey meat.

Pour into 4 small ovenproof bowls. Sprinkle with nutmeg. Set bowls in shallow pan half full with water, and bake for 30 minutes.

TOTAL GRAMS   9.8
GRAMS PER SERVING   2.7

Roast Turkey

Preheat oven to 400° F.

This is an easy delicious way to cook a perfect, moist turkey. Have turkey at room temperature. Remove giblets from cavity. Run turkey under cold water to clean inside and out. Never soak a turkey in water. Dry turkey well. Rub turkey with garlic inside and out. Place sliced oranges and lemons in the cavity if you are not stuffing it or use the Almond Stuffing that follows. Insert poultry pins to draw open cavity together. Use string to lace between pins as you would lace a boot.

Tie legs together with string if not already tucked under a piece of string. Bend wing tips under body and tuck loose neck skin under turkey.

Place turkey breast side up in a stainless-steel roasting pan that has a cover. Cover turkey breast with slices of turkey bacon. Place cover on pan.

Bake at 400° F. for 20 minutes. Reduce to 350° F. Cook for 15 minutes per pound if turkey is over 10 pounds. If under 10 pounds, cook for 20 minutes per pound. If a turkey is stuffed and over 10 pounds, cook for 20 minutes per pound.

TOTAL GRAMS   0

Almond Stuffing

12 ¼-cup servings

½ cup butter
½ cut finely chopped onion
¼ pound smoked ham, chopped fine
¼ cup chopped parsley
½ teaspoon thyme
½ teaspoon freshly ground pepper
½ cup fried pork rinds, crushed
2 eggs
¼ cup dry red wine
⅔ cup blanched almonds

Melt butter in large skillet. Add onions. Cook until light brown. Add ham, parsley, and spices. Mix well. Combine mixture with pork rinds, eggs, wine, and almonds.

Use to stuff chicken, turkey, veal roast, or anything that needs a stuffing.

TOTAL GRAMS 41.6
GRAMS PER SERVING 3.5

Duck in Red Wine

4 servings

2 tablespoons butter or rendered chicken fat
1 5–6 pound duck, skin removed and cut into 8 pieces
2 cups dry red wine
8 shiitake mushrooms
2 sprigs parsley, minced
1 small bay leaf
⅛ teaspoon thyme
1 teaspoon seasoned salt
8 small white onions, peeled
2 carrots, peeled and quartered

Preheat oven to 350° F.

Melt butter in a large skillet. Brown pieces of duck in fat over a medium heat.

Remove to a 9-inch casserole.

Add garlic to fat and cook 1 minute. Add red wine, shiitake mushrooms, parsley, bay leaf, thyme, and salt. Bring to a boil, stirring constantly until sauce thickens. Place onions and carrots into casserole with duck. Top with sauce.

Cover and bake for 1¼ hours.

TOTAL GRAMS 67.8
GRAMS PER SERVING 16.9

Hal's Chicken

4 servings

1 chicken, cut into 8 pieces
Mustard Sauce *to cover*
1 medium onion, sliced thin
1 medium tomato, sliced thin
2 tablespoons fresh dill, minced
seasoned salt to taste

Preheat oven 350° F.
　　Wash and dry chicken. Place in a baking dish and cover with *Mustard Sauce.* Top with onion slices and then tomatoes. Sprinkle with dill and salt.
　　　　Cover and bake for 1 hour. Remove lid and bake 1 hour more.

TOTAL GRAMS　　31.5
GRAMS PER SERVING　　7.9

Joan's Chicken Mascarpone

4 servings

4 boneless chicken breasts
2 medium onions, sliced thin
3 cloves garlic, minced
½ teaspoon dried tarragon
3 tablespoons dry white wine
3 tablespoons mascarpone cheese

Preheat oven 350° F.
　　Place chicken breasts in a glass baking dish. Sauté onions, garlic, and tarragon until onions become golden. Place on top of chicken.

Swish wine in sauté pan and add mascarpone cheese. Allow cheese to melt (about 30 seconds), stir well to combine flavors and spoon over chicken and onions. Cover.

Bake for 1 hour.

TOTAL GRAMS	16.8
GRAMS PER SERVING	4.2

Tandoori Chicken

4 servings

1 5-pound chicken, cut in 8 pieces
4 cloves garlic
2-inch piece ginger, peeled
2 bay leaves
2 teaspoons chili powder
1 teaspoon sea salt
2 teaspoons tumeric
1 teaspoon coriander, ground
½ teaspoon cumin
½ teaspoon cinnamon, ground
½ teaspoon cloves, ground
¼ cup olive oil
1½ cups sour cream
juice of 2 lemons

Preheat oven to 350° F.

Place chicken in a glass baking dish large enough for pieces to lie side by side.

Place all 10 spices in a blender and grind to a paste.

Combine spices with sour cream and lemon juice.

Dip each piece of chicken into the mixture and coat it completely. Return chicken to baking dish.

Place in refrigerator to marinate overnight.

Bake chicken for 45 minutes.

TOTAL GRAMS	31.4
GRAMS PER SERVING	7.8

Goat Cheesy Chicken Rolls

4 servings

4 chicken breasts, pounded thin
½ cup goat cheese, crumbled
½ cup fresh basil, minced
1 tablespoon sun-dried tomatoes, softened in olive oil and minced
¼ small onion, minced
½ teaspoon oregano
½ teaspoon seasoned salt
¼ cup dry white wine

Preheat oven 350° F.

Oil a small glass baking dish.

In a small bowl combine all ingredients except chicken and blend well. Spread mixture on chicken breasts and roll them. Fasten with a toothpick. Arrange in baking dish so rolled breasts do not touch each other. Pour wine over chicken rolls.

Bake for 45 minutes.

TOTAL GRAMS   32.0
GRAMS PER SERVING   8.0

Oriental Chicken with Broccoli Rabe

4 servings

3 teaspoons olive oil
2 teaspoons sesame oil
2 teaspoons ginger, minced
2 teaspoons garlic, minced
4 deboned chicken breasts, cubed
4 large shiitake mushrooms
2 whole scallions, minced
8 ounces broccoli rabe, cut into 2-inch lengths
1 tablespoon Tamari soy sauce
2 tablespoons dry sherry

Heat 2 teaspoons of olive oil and 2 teaspoons sesame oil in a nonstick wok or skillet. Do not allow oil to smoke. Add ginger and garlic and stir for 30 seconds. Add chicken and mushrooms and stir 3 minutes more. Remove from skillet. Stir remaining olive oil into skillet. Add scallions and broccoli rabe. Stir-fry for 1 minute. Put back chicken and mushrooms and add soy sauce and wine.

Remove chicken and vegetables with a slotted spoon. Place on a serving plate. Boil sauce until it reduces by half. Pour over chicken and serve immediately.

TOTAL GRAMS 43.1
GRAMS PER SERVING 10.8

Turkey Sausage Patties

8 patties

2 tablespoons garlic oil
1 small onion, chopped fine
1 clove garlic, minced
1 pound turkey, ground
3 tablespoons sour cream
10 pork rinds, crushed
½ teaspoon sage, minced
½ teaspoon seasoned salt
2 tablespoons walnut oil

Heat garlic oil in a nonstick skillet. Add onion and garlic and sauté until onions are golden.

Mix all other ingredients (except walnut oil) together in a bowl. Add onions and garlic and shape into eight balls. Flatten balls into patties. Heat walnut oil in skillet and sauté patties until brown on both sides.

TOTAL GRAMS 35.5
GRAMS PER SERVING 4.4

Ivan's Crisp Chicken

4 servings

1 5-pound chicken, cut in 8 pieces
4 tablespoons garlic oil
¼ cup white wine
1 medium-size red onion, sliced thin
seasoned salt to taste
¼ cup grated Jarlsberg cheese
¼ cup grated sharp Cheddar cheese

Preheat oven to 350° F.

Wash and dry chicken. Brush with garlic oil. Place in baking dish and sprinkle with wine. Cover with onions. Salt to taste and bake, covered, for ½ hour.

Uncover, sprinkle with cheeses and bake until chicken, onions, and cheeses are crisp, about 45 minutes.

TOTAL GRAMS 10.6
GRAMS PER SERVING 2.6

Fish and Shellfish

Sun Luck Scallops

4 servings

¼ cup Tamari soy sauce
⅛ cup sake
1 pound bay scallops
2 tablespoons sesame oil
6 shiitake mushrooms, slivered
½ cup sour cream

Preheat oven to 350° F.

Mix soy sauce and sake together. Place scallops in a glass baking dish. Pour soy sauce mixture over scallops and place in refrigerator for ½ hour. Heat sesame oil in a skillet. Sauté slivered mushrooms for 2 minutes. Turn off heat and allow to cool in oil. Place scallops in oven and bake for 10 minutes. Spoon sour cream into a small dish. Spoon 1 tablespoon of sauce from scallops over mushrooms and artfully arrange them on top of sour cream. Enjoy eating by taking a small amount of mushroom and sour cream on a fork, then adding a scallop.

TOTAL GRAMS   36.2
GRAMS PER SERVING   9.1

Snappy Swordfish

6 servings

2½ pounds swordfish steak
juice of 1 lemon
3 teaspoons garlic paste (available in a tube)
2 tablespoons fresh dill (or 1 tablespoon dried, minced)
1 medium tomato, thinly sliced
½ pound shiitake mushrooms, sliced
3 tablespoons olive oil
¼ cup sunflower seeds
½ pound snap peas
¼ cup dry white wine
3 ounces herbed goat cheese, crumbled

Preheat oven at 350° F.

Wash and dry swordfish. Sprinkle both sides with lemon juice and place in a glass baking dish.

Spread garlic paste on fish, covering it completely. Top with dill, tomato, and mushrooms. Sprinkle olive oil and sunflower seeds evenly across the top.

Cut ends off of snap peas. Spread over fish.

Pour wine over the peas.

Cover top of dish tightly with aluminum foil and place in oven for 20 minutes. Uncover, add goat cheese and cook for 10 minutes more. Baste fish during last 10 minutes.

TOTAL GRAMS 42.0
GRAMS PER SERVING 7.0

Poached Fish Fillets (Basic Recipe)

4 servings

4 fish fillets (sole, halibut or flounder)
juice of 1 lemon
1 small onion
seasoned salt
1 tablespoon butter
2 mushrooms, thinly sliced
¼ cup water
½ cup dry white wine

Preheat oven to 350° F.

Wash and dry fillets in a mixture of water and lemon juice. Place in a glass baking dish. Melt butter in a pan. Add mushrooms and shake to cover mushrooms with butter. Sprinkle with ½ teaspoon seasoned salt. Cook for 2 minutes. Stir in water and wine. Bring to a boil and pour over fish. Cover, place in oven and poach for 15 minutes. For salmon allow to cook 5 minutes more.

TOTAL GRAMS 13.1
GRAMS PER SERVING 3.3

Halibut Roll-Ups

6 servings

2 pounds fillet of halibut
seasoned salt
3 slices bacon, diced
¼ pound shiitake mushrooms, sliced
¼ cup celery, diced
2 tablespoons onion, diced
1 clove galic, minced
1 tablespoon parsley, minced
3 tablespoons sweet butter, melted
½ cup dry white wine
¼ cup grated Parmesan cheese
paprika to taste

Preheat oven to 350° F.

Sprinkle fillets with salt. Allow to stand for about 10 minutes. Place in a glass baking dish.

In skillet, sauté bacon, mushrooms, celery, and onion until vegetables are soft and bacon is crisp. Add garlic and cook 2 minutes more. Add parsley, and blend well.

Spread mixture over fillets, roll up, and fasten with toothpicks.

Place 1 tablespoon melted butter in bottom of baking dish. Add fish.

Pour remaining butter over fish, and add wine.

Sprinkle with Parmesan cheese and paprika.

Bake for ½ hour.

TOTAL GRAMS 21.4
GRAMS PER SERVING 3.6

Chinese Fish Balls

6 servings

2 pounds of white fish (carp, haddock, scrod, bass), chopped fine
1 egg
1 teaspoon salt
4 tablespoons sesame oil
3 tablespoons of water
½ green pepper, sliced thin
5 water chestnuts, sliced thin
6 shiitake mushroom caps, sliced
2 cloves garlic, minced
walnut oil for deep frying
½ cup bean sprouts
2 teaspoons ginger, minced
pinch of sugar substitute
⅛ cup Chicken Stock

Prepare chopped fish in food processor. Beat egg and salt together with 1 tablespoon sesame oil and water. Add fish and form into ½-inch balls. In skillet, heat the walnut oil until very hot. Deep fry fish balls for 2 minutes. They will be light brown. Remove from fat with a slotted spoon and drain on paper toweling. Heat a pot of water to boiling. Reduce to a simmer. Drop fish balls into boiling water for 2 minutes. Remove with slotted spoon and set aside. (Up until now you can make them in advance and store in refrigerator).

Place 3 tablespoons of sesame oil in a wok. Heat oil until hot. Add peppers, water chestnuts, mushrooms, garlic, bean sprouts, and ginger. Sprinkle with salt and sugar substitute. Stir-fry for 2 to 3 minutes, reduce heat. Add *Chicken Stock* and fish balls. Stir well, and serve.

TOTAL GRAMS 24.7
GRAMS PER SERVING 4.1

Fabulous Flounder

6 servings

3 pounds flounder fillets
lemon juice
salt and pepper
1 teaspoon dried tarragon
2 cups sour cream
1 tablespoon minced chives and parsley

Preheat oven to 350° F.

Oil a baking dish just large enough to hold fish fillets. Rub fillets with lemon juice, salt, and pepper, and place in dish.

Sprinkle with tarragon. Cover with sour cream and bake for 15 minutes.

Remove from oven, and sprinkle with chives and parsley. Serve immediately.

TOTAL GRAMS 21.4
GRAMS PER SERVING 3.6

Stuffed Flounder

6 servings

2 pounds fillet of flounder
salt, to taste
3 slices bacon, diced
¼ pound shiitake mushrooms, sliced
¼ cup diced celery
2 tablespoons diced onion
1 clove garlic, diced fine
1 tablespoon parsley, minced
3 tablespoons butter, melted
½ cup dry white wine
¼ cup grated Parmesan cheese
paprika

Preheat oven to 350° F.

Sprinkle fillets with salt. Allow to stand for about 10 minutes.

Sauté bacon, mushrooms, celery, and onion in a nonstick skillet until vegetables are soft and bacon crisp. Add garlic. Cook for 2 minutes more. Add parsley, and blend well.

Spread mixture over fillets, roll them up, and fasten with toothpicks. Place 1 tablespoon melted butter in bottom of baking dish. Add fish.

Pour remaining butter over fish, and add wine.

Sprinkle with Parmesan cheese and paprika.

Bake for ½ hour.

TOTAL GRAMS 21.4
GRAMS PER SERVING 3.6

Fennel Red Snapper

4 servings

4 fillets of red snapper
½ stick of butter, at room temperature
¼ teaspoon fennel seeds
½ teaspoon lemon juice
¼ teaspoon dried tarragon
¼ clove garlic, minced
seasoned salt to taste
¼ cup olive oil
1 teaspoon grated lemon rind
½ bay leaf

Preheat oven to 350° F.

Wash and dry fish. Combine butter, fennel seeds, lemon juice, tarragon, garlic, and salt. Spread butter mixture on fish fillets, roll them up, and fasten with toothpicks.

Combine oil, lemon rind, and bay leaf in baking dish. Add fish and marinate in refrigerator for 1 hour. Turn once. Drain fish and reserve marinade.

Bake for 45 minutes. Serve with warmed marinade on side.

TOTAL GRAMS 3.0
GRAMS PER SERVING 0.8

Trout in Tomato Sauce

4 servings

2 good-size trout
5 tablespoons tomato sauce
8 tablespoons cider vinegar
3 tablespoons olive oil
1 tablespoon minced onion
4 drops Tabasco sauce (optional)
1 pinch sugar substitute

Clean and fillet trout, and cut into ½-inch pieces. Arrange attractively in shallow serving dish.

Combine remaining ingredients. Mix well. Pour over fish and cover. Place in refrigerator for 24 hours.

Variation: If you prefer herring and it is available, use same recipe. After filleting herring, place in shallow bowl, and add enough cold tea to cover. Refrigerate overnight to remove excess salt. Follow remaining recipe.

TOTAL GRAMS   9.7
GRAMS PER SERVING   2.4

Fresh Spring Salmon Mousse

10 servings

2 envelopes unflavored gelatin
1½ cups cold water
⅔ cup sour cream
1 cup mayonnaise
1½ pounds fresh salmon, cooked, skinned, and boned
½ teaspoon onion powder
1 tablespoon capers
2 teaspoons dill
1 cup cucumbers, chopped and peeled
1 teaspoon salt

Soften gelatin in cold water. Heat until completely dissolved. Cool.

Mix sour cream and mayonnaise together. Add gelatin, and chill until slightly thickened.

Flake salmon and add onion powder, capers, dill, cucumbers, and salt. Mix well with sour cream and mayonnaise.

Pour into 5-cup mold. Refrigerate until firm.

Unmold and serve.

TOTAL GRAMS   19.6
GRAMS PER SERVING   2.0

Tuna Loaf

6 servings

2 cups canned tuna or 1 pound fresh tuna, poached
2 teaspoons diced onion
2 teaspoons capers
1 cup mayonnaise
½ cup water
½ cup heavy cream
½ teaspoon salt
¼ teaspoon paprika
½ teaspoon curry, or to taste

Preheat oven to 350° F.

Drain fish. In a small bowl flake fish. Add onion and capers to fish.

In a saucepan combine mayonnaise, water, cream, salt, and paprika. Stir until smooth.

Add half of cream sauce to fish and mix. Place mixture in buttered loaf pan or baking dish. Bake for 30 minutes.

Add curry to remaining sauce. To serve, slice fish loaf and spoon sauce over slices.

TOTAL GRAMS 9.9
GRAMS PER SERVING 1.6

Oriental Shrimp

2 servings

2 tablespoons butter
2 tablespoons onion, chopped
3 slices boiled ham
1 clove garlic, minced
½ cup bean sprouts
¼ head cabbage, shredded
1 pound raw shrimp, shelled and deveined
4 servings Fish Stock

Preheat oven to 350° F.

Melt butter in saucepan, add onion, and sauté until soft. Add ham and garlic, and sauté for 3 minutes. Add bean sprouts, and sauté for about 3 or 4 minutes until lightly browned.

Place shrimp in small casserole. Add uncooked cabbage to bean sprout mixture. Spread over shrimp.

Pour *Fish Stock* over shrimp. Sprinkle with paprika. Cover dish with lid or aluminum foil and bake for 30 minutes.

TOTAL GRAMS 14.2
GRAMS PER SERVING 3.6

Shrimp Parmesan

4 servings

2 pounds raw shrimp, shelled and deveined
2 tablespoons olive oil
½ cup onion, minced
2 cloves garlic, minced
8 ounces tomato sauce
½ cup clam broth
1 teaspoon basil
¼ teaspoon oregano
2 teaspoons salt
pepper to taste
¼ cup grated Parmesan cheese
8 ounces shredded mozzarella cheese

Preheat broiler.

Heat oil in skillet. Sauté onion until golden, add garlic, and sauté 1 minute.

Add shrimp and sauté for 3 minutes.

In skillet, heat remainder of oil until light brown. Add tomato sauce and oregano. Simmer for 15 minutes.

Pour over shrimp and add shredded mozzarella cheese on top. Sprinkle Parmesan as final layer and broil until bubbly.

TOTAL GRAMS 17.6
GRAMS PER SERVING 4.4

Shrimps and Scallops Marc

6 servings

½ pound medium shrimp, shelled and deveined
dash seasoned salt
dash garlic powder
1 egg, beaten
¼ cup grated Parmesan cheese
½ pound sea scallops

¼ cup heavy cream
2 tablespoons sweet butter
3 strips bacon, quartered
¼ cup dry white wine
¼ cup heavy cream
tarragon

Sprinkle shrimp with salt and garlic powder. Dip shrimp in egg and then coat with Parmesan cheese.

Sprinkle scallops with salt and garlic powder, dip into heavy cream and then coat with Parmesan cheese.

Melt butter in pan. Add bacon, scallops, and shrimp. Brown on both sides; add wine and simmer for 10 minutes. Add cream and simmer gently for 10 minutes longer. Garnish with tarragon.

TOTAL GRAMS   9.4
GRAMS PER SERVING   4.7

Broiled Tarragon Lobster Tails

2 servings

4 frozen lobster tails
½ stick butter
1 tablespoon fresh chopped ginger (or ½ tablespoon dried)
1 teaspoon dried tarragon
½ teaspoon dry mustard
seasoned salt

Preheat broiler.

Remove soft part of lobster tail with scissors. Hit hard shell slightly with mallet or cleaver to make it lie flat. Melt butter. Add ginger, tarragon, mustard, and salt. Spoon generously over tails and let stand in marinade for several hours. Remove from marinade.

Broil about 4 inches from heat for 10–15 minutes with meaty side up. Baste often.

TOTAL GRAMS   2.1
GRAMS PER SERVING   1.1

Crabmeat Almond Pie

8 servings

¼ cup chopped toasted almonds (see Toasted Nuts *recipe)*
2 eggs plus 2 yolks
2 teaspoons Dijon mustard
2 teaspoon seasoned salt
2 tablespoon chives, minced
2 cups grated fontina cheese
4 ounces frozen or canned crabmeat
1½ cups heavy cream

Preheat oven to 300° F.

Place toasted almonds on the bottom of 9-inch pie plate.

Put eggs in bowl and beat well. Add mustard, salt, chives, cheese, and crabmeat.

Scald heavy cream by bringing it right to a boiling point (do not boil).

Add heavy cream to crabmeat mixture and pour into pie plate.

Bake for 1 hour.

TOTAL GRAMS   40.7
GRAMS PER SERVING   5.1

Curried Crabmeat

4 servings

1 pound crabmeat, flaked and picked over for bones
¾ cup onion, chopped
¼ cup olive oil
2 tablespoons curry powder
2 tablespoons fresh parsley, minced
¼ teaspoon crushed red pepper
2 tablespoons lemon juice
½ teaspoon seasoned salt
½ teaspoon black pepper
¼ teaspoon oregano
½ cup grated Parmesan cheese
2 tablespoons butter
1 lemon, cut into wedges

Preheat broiler.

Sauté onion in oil until soft. Add curry powder and cook, stirring constantly, for 1 minute.

Stir in crabmeat, parsley, and red pepper, and sauté for 2 minutes. Add lemon juice, salt, pepper, and oregano. Sauté for 1 minute more.

Divide crabmeat mixture among 4 buttered scallop shells, sprinkle each serving with Parmesan cheese, and dot tops with butter. Put shells under broiler for 2–3 minutes, or until cheese is golden. Serve shells with wedges of lemon.

TOTAL GRAMS 29.4
GRAMS PER SERVING 9.6

Houston's Cerviche

4 servings

1 pound fresh whitefish cut in bite-size pieces
½ pound medium shrimp, shelled and deveined
½ pound bay scallops
juice of 6 limes
juice of 4 lemons
3 tablespoons garlic, minced
6 slices ginger root, peeled
1 medium onion, sliced thin
1 teaspoon cilantro, minced

Wash and dry fish and shellfish. Mix all remaining ingredients together. Place in a glass baking dish just large enough to fit fish, shrimp, and scallops. Mix fish, shellfish, and citrus mixture and refrigerate for 2 days until fish and shellfish "cook." The fish and shellfish will be opaque and appear to have been cooked.

Serve cold or at room temperature.

TOTAL GRAMS 68.8
GRAMS PER SERVING 17.0

Pasta

Manicotti

12 crepes

½ recipe Pasta Sauce
1 recipe Pasta

Stuffing for Pasta
1 pound ricotta cheese
6 ounces mozzarella cheese
2 teaspoons parsley
5 tablespoons grated Parmesan cheese
2 eggs

Preheat oven to 300° F.

Prepare 7 cups *Pasta Sauce* and 12 *Pasta Crepes.*

In a bowl mix ricotta cheese, mozzarella cheese, parsley, 2 tablespoons Parmesan cheese, and eggs.

Cover the bottom of large baking pan with thin layer of *Pasta Sauce.*

Place about 2 full tablespoons of ricotta mixture in center of crepe. Roll crepe around stuffing like large noodle. Place crepe in baking pan, seam side down. Repeat with each crepe, placing them side by side in baking pan. Pour remaining sauce over crepes.

Sprinkle remaining 3 tablespoons Parmesan cheese on top. Bake for 20 minutes.

TOTAL GRAMS 64.8
GRAMS PER MANICOTTI 7.2

Gnocchi

8 servings

1 pound ricotta cheese, pressed of liquid
½ pound cream cheese or Boursin cheese
3 eggs, beaten
2 tablespoons soy flour
dash of salt, cayenne pepper, and nutmeg
½ pound sweet butter, melted
½ cup grated Parmesan cheese

Push ricotta cheese and cream cheese through a fine strainer. (The easiest and fastest way is with your hands.)

Beat eggs into mixture with electric or rotary beater. Blend in soy flour and seasonings. Refrigerate for about 1 hour. Bring large pot of water to rolling boil. Lower heat to simmer. Drop cheese mixture into water by teaspoonfuls. (They will drop and then rise to the top.)

Allow gnocchi to poach (simmer on top of water) for about 20 minutes. Remove gnocchi carefully with a slotted spoon and allow to drain on paper towel.

Melt ¼ pound butter in large baking dish. Place drained gnocchi in dish. Cover with remaining melted butter and grated Parmesan cheese.

Gnocchi may be served immediately, kept warm in a low oven or refrigerated and reheated.

The substition of Boursin for cream chees will give you a much spicer gnocchi. Adding ¼ packages of frozen spinach that has been thawed and dried makes a delicious Spinach Gnocchi.

TOTAL GRAMS 32.0
GRAMS PER SERVING 4.0

Enchiladas

6 servings

1 recipe Pasta
1½ pounds pork, ground
3 cloves garlic, minced
3 teaspoons chili powder
3 tablespoons cider vinegar
1 tablespoon oil
3 tablespoons chopped onion
1 8-ounce can tomato sauce
1 can water
½ teaspoon cumin
6 drops Tabasco sauce, or to taste
1 teaspoon salt, or to taste
1½ cups shredded Cheddar cheese

Prepare *Pasta* recipe. Place *Pasta* on wax paper, and set aside to be filled later. This can be made a day ahead and stored in refrigerator with wax paper separating crepes.

Preheat oven to 350° F.

In bowl combine ground pork, garlic, 2 teaspoons chili powder, and vinegar.

Heat oil in skillet, and sauté onions on medium heat for 3 or 4 minutes until soft.

Form pork mixture into 1 large ball and place in skillet with onion. As pork is browning, slowly break into small pieces. Cook thoroughly. Pour off all fat. Set aside.

Sauce:

In saucepan combine tomato sauce, water, cumin, 1 teaspoon chili powder, Tabasco sauce, and salt. Simmer for ½ hour.

In baking pan 13×9 inches, pour ½ cup sauce. Spoon heaping tablespoon shredded cheese. Fold over and place crepes side by side in baking pan. Repeat until you use all crepes. Pour remaining sauce over all crepes. Bake for 15 minutes. Cover with remaining cheese. Bake for 5 minutes more or until cheese is hot and bubbly.

TOTAL GRAMS 39.5
GRAMS PER SERVING 6.6

Pasta

12 crepes

⅓ cup soy flour
½ cup water
3 eggs
1 tablespoon oil

Put all ingredients in blender. Blend until smooth. Use a crepe pan or a 5- or 6-inch skillet. Cover bottom of pan lightly with small amount of oil. When pan is hot enough to sizzle a drop of water, pour about 3 tablespoons of crepe mixture into pan. Tilt pan to distribute mixture evenly. Crepes should be thin. Lightly brown on both sides (about 1 minute on each side). Place on wax paper until all crepes are finished.

The crepes are very delicate, so handle carefully. If you have trouble the first time, try again. Oil pan again if necessary.

They could be made a day ahead and stored in refrigerator separated by wax paper.

TOTAL GRAMS 24.6
GRAMS PER CREPE 2.1

Cannelloni

4 servings

3 chicken livers
1 boned chicken breast
4 tablespoons butter
5 slices prosciutto ham
¼ teaspoon marjoram
¾ cup grated Parmesan cheese
1 recipe Cream Sauce
8 crepes Pasta *recipe*

Sauté chicken livers and chicken breast in butter until brown on both sides. Grind livers, chicken breast, and prosciutto in food grinder with medium blade. Mix in marjoram and ½ cup grated Parmesan cheese. Add 10 tablespoons *Cream Sauce.* Place 2 tablespoons chicken mixture in center of each crepe. Roll up crepes.

Butter baking dish, and place crepes side by side. Cover with remaining cream sauce and Parmesan cheese. Bake for 1½ hours.

TOTAL GRAMS   29.8
GRAMS PER SERVING   3.7

Bread

4 Grain and Seed Bread

12 slices

1 tablespoon unbleached flour
1 tablespoon whole wheat flour
1 tablespoon sesame seeds
1 tablespoon cornmeal
½ teaspoon baking powder
2 eggs, separated
1 packet sugar substitute
⅛ teaspoon seasoned salt
2 tablespoons ricotta cheese, whole milk
2 tablespoons butter
⅛ teaspoon cream of tartar
1 tablespoon pumpkin seeds

Preheat oven to 350° F.

Mix flours, seeds, cornmeal, and baking powder together. Beat in egg yolks. Sprinkle with sugar substitute and seasoned salt. Mix cheese with butter. Add dry ingredients to cheese mixture and blend well.

Beat egg whites with cream of tartar until stiff. Fold into cheese mixture.

Spoon into a small, oiled loaf pan. Sprinkle with pumpkin seeds and bake for 50 minutes. Cool on a wire rack.

TOTAL GRAMS 18.5
GRAMS PER SERVING 1.5

Rye Bread

12 slices

2 tablespoons unbleached flour
1 tablespoon whole wheat flour
1 tablespoon caraway seeds
½ teaspoon baking powder
1 packet sugar substitute
2 eggs, separated
⅛ teaspoon seasoned salt
2 tablespoons ricotta cheese
2 tablespoons butter, melted
⅛ teaspoon cream of tartar

Preheat oven to 350° F.

Mix flours and caraway seeds together. Beat in egg yolks and sprinkle with seasoned salt and sugar substitute. Mix cheese with butter, add dry ingredients, and blend well. Beat egg whites with cream of tartar until stiff. Spoon into a small oiled loaf pan and bake for 50 minutes. Remove from oven and cool on rack.

TOTAL GRAMS 25.5
GRAMS PER SERVING 2.1

Zucchini Bread

12 slices

2 tablespoons unbleached flour
1 tablespoon whole wheat flour
1 cup zucchini, grated and pressed to remove liquid
½ teaspoon baking powder
¼ teaspoon seasoned salt
1 packet sugar substitute
2 eggs, separated
2 tablespoons ricotta cheese
2 tablespoons grated Parmesan cheese
⅛ teaspoon cream of tartar
10 walnuts

Preheat oven to 350° F.

Mix flours, salt, sugar substitute, and zucchini. Beat in one egg yolk at a time. Mix in ricotta and Parmesan cheeses. Beat egg whites until stiff with cream of tartar. Spoon into small loaf pan and place walnut halves on top.

Bake for 50 minutes. Remove from oven and cool on a rack.

TOTAL GRAMS 24.0
GRAMS PER SERVING 2.0

Vegetables

Eggplant Parmigiana

8 servings

1 large eggplant, cut into ½-inch slices
4 tablespoons olive oil
1 large onion, chopped
2 cloves garlic, minced
1 pound chuck, ground
1 8-ounce can tomato sauce
1 cup water
1 teaspoon oregano
½ cup grated Parmesan cheese
1 8-ounce package mozzarella cheese, sliced

Preheat oven to 350° F.

Soak eggplant in salted water for 1 hour. Dry with paper towels.

Heat 2 tablespoons olive oil in a skillet and lightly brown chopped onion. Add garlic and sauté one more minute. Add ground chuck, stir and cook. When meat turns brown, add tomato sauce and water. Simmer for 15 minutes. Place remaining olive oil in a large skillet on medium heat, and sauté a few eggplant slices at a time until golden brown; add a little more oil if needed.

Oil a baking dish and arrange half of the eggplant slices on the bottom. Cover with half of the tomato mixture. Sprinkle with half of the Parmesan cheese and half of the mozzarella. Repeat these layers.

Bake for 25 to 30 minutes until golden brown.

TOTAL GRAMS 20.6
GRAMS PER SERVING 2.6

Broccoli in Cheese Sauce

6 servings

1 pound broccoli
1 recipe Cheese Sauce

Prepare broccoli by removing hard stem and reserving florets. Place in a steamer and steam for 10 to 15 minutes depending on how soft you like your vegetables. Serve with *Cheese Sauce* (3 tablespoons per serving).

TOTAL GRAMS 36.7
GRAMS PER SERVING 6.1

Baked Spinach

4 servings

¾ cup spinach (½ frozen package or 3 cups fresh)
¼ cup water
3 tablespoons olive oil
3 tablespoons butter
3 tablespoons minced onion
1 clove garlic, minced
2 slices prosciutto, diced
5 eggs
3 tablespoons heavy cream
pinch of black pepper
3 tablespoons grated Parmesan cheese

Preheat oven to 350° F.
    Wash spinach well. Be careful to remove all sand. Do not dry.
    Place spinach in saucepan with water, cover, and steam for about 6 minutes. Drain.
    Heat olive oil and butter in skillet.
    Add onion, garlic, and proscuitto to skillet. Cook slowly until onion is light brown. Add onion mixture to spinach. Simmer for 5 minutes.

Beat eggs with cream, and add pepper. Add spinach mixture and Parmesan cheese to eggs.

Lightly oil an 8-inch-square baking dish. Place mixture in dish, and bake for 30 minutes. Cut into 4 squares.

TOTAL GRAMS 16.5
GRAMS PER SERVING 4.5

Stuffed Zippy Zucchini

4 servings

2 medium-size zucchini
3 ounces ricotta cheese
1 teaspoon minced parsley
1 onion, chopped
1 egg white, beaten stiff
1 8-ounce can tomato sauce

Preheat oven to 300° F.

Cut zucchini into halves lengthwise and scoop out pulp.

Combine ricotta, parsley, and onion. Mix well. Fold in egg white.

Stuff mixture into halved zucchini. Place in baking dish and pour tomato sauce over top.

Bake for 10 minutes. Lower heat to 250° F. and cook for 30 more minutes. Baste often.

TOTAL GRAMS 35.2
GRAMS PER SERVING 8.8

Zucchini Stuffed with Cream Sauce

6 servings

6 medium-size zucchini
3 tablespoons mayonnaise
2 tablespoons grated Parmesan cheese
½ cup sliced mushrooms
4 slices lean prosciutto, diced
1 egg yolk
1 teaspoon salt
½ teaspoon pepper
½ teaspoon oregano
3 tablespoons olive oil

Preheat oven to 375° F.

In large pot of boiling water, add zucchini and boil for 5 minutes. Remove from heat, and cut zucchini into halves lengthwise. Scoop out pulp and save.

Mix together pulp from zucchini, mayonnaise, Parmesan cheese, mushrooms, prosciutto, egg yolk, salt, pepper, and oregano.

Place zucchini halves in greased baking dish and fill each zucchini half with mixture. Sprinkle with olive oil. Bake for 30 minutes.

TOTAL GRAMS   29.9
GRAMS PER SERVING   5.0

String Beans Almandine

4 servings

1 pound fresh or frozen string beans
½ pound shiitake mushrooms, sliced
4 tablespoons butter
½ teaspoon seasoned salt
¼ cup slivered almonds

Prepare string beans for cooking. Simmer in small amount of water for 10 minutes. In a skillet sauté mushrooms in butter until brown. Add salt and almonds.

Add string beans to skillet. Toss well. Simmer for 4 minutes. Correct seasoning to taste.

Total Grams 48.0
Grams per Serving 12.0

Mock Potato Dumplings

12 dumplings

½ head cauliflower (1 cup mashed)
2 eggs, beaten
½ cup grated Parmesan cheese
1 teaspoon parsley
1 teaspoon nutmeg
4 tablespoons soy flour
1 tablespoon salt
4 tablespoons butter

Boil cauliflower until soft, for about 25 minutes. Mash with fork or potato masher.

Add eggs, Parmesan cheese, parsley, nutmeg, and soy flour. Shape into walnut-size balls.

Bring large pot of water to rolling boil. Add salt. Drop cauliflower balls into water. When they rise, remove with slotted spoon.

Heat butter in skillet. Fry balls until brown on all sides. Drain on paper towel.

Total Grams 45.3
Grams per Dumpling 3.1

Chinese Snow Pea Pods

6 servings

2 tablespoons vegetable oil
1 onion, chopped fine
1 clove garlic, chopped fine
½ teaspoon seasoned salt
¼ cup sliced water chestnuts
½ pound snow pea pods
1 tablespoon Tamari soy sauce
¼ cup Chicken Stock

Heat oil in heavy skillet. Add onion, garlic, salt, and water chestnuts. Sauté until onion is golden. Add pea pods, soy sauce, and *Chicken Stock*. Cover and cook for 5 minutes. Uncover and cook for 5 more minutes.

TOTAL GRAMS   31.8
GRAMS PER SERVING   5.3

Eggplant Little Shoes

8 servings

4 medium eggplants
2 tablespoons butter
4 tablespoons onion
1 clove garlic
1 pound beef or lamb, chopped
1 8-ounce can tomato sauce
1 teaspoon cumin
1 teaspoon parsley
1 teaspoon seasoned salt
pepper to taste
1 egg
1 tablespoon water
1 tablespoon lemon juice
¼ cup grated Parmesan cheese

Preheat oven to 350° F.

Wash eggplants. Do not peel. Parboil whole eggplants in salted boiling water for 5 minutes. Remove. Cut in half lengthwise. Spoon out center pulp carefully and chop, leaving about ¼-inch around rim.

Melt butter in saucepan. Add onion and garlic. Sauté for 3 minutes. Add meat and eggplant pulp. Stir. Brown lightly. Add tomato sauce, cumin, parsley, salt, and pepper. Cook over low heat until all liquid is absorbed.

Place eggplants in lightly oiled roasting pan or large casserole dish. Stuff with chopped meat mixture. Beat egg, water, and lemon juice together. Pour over eggplants. Sprinkle with Parmesan cheese. Bake for 20 minutes until lightly browned.

TOTAL GRAMS 60.5
GRAMS PER SERVING 7.5

Cheese-Stuffed Eggplant

8 servings

4 medium-size eggplants
2 medium-size onions
3 tablespoons butter
3 cups crumbled feta cheese
½ cup grated Parmesan cheese
¼ cup ricotta cheese
1 egg
2 tablespoons chopped parsley
seasoned salt

Preheat oven to 350° F.

Slice eggplants in half. Scoop out pulp, chop it, and set aside. Reserve shells. Sauté onions in butter until golden. Add eggplant pulp and continue to sauté for about 5 more minutes. Transfer mixture to bowl and let cool. Add cheeses to mixture, and beat in egg and parsley. Sprinkle on salt. Stuff mixture in eggplant shells. Bake for 40 minutes.

TOTAL GRAMS 62.1
GRAMS PER SERVING 6.8

The Most Delicious Cucumbers

4 servings

4 cucumbers, peeled and seeded
½ tablespoon seasoned salt
½ tablespoon tarragon vinegar
¼ cup butter, melted
1 tablespoon minced dill
1 tablespoon minced chives
1 tablespoon minced onion
¼ cup heavy cream
2 tablespoons minced parsley
grated Parmesan cheese

Preheat oven to 375° F.

Slice cucumbers to bite-size pieces. Add salt and vinegar. Allow to stand at room temperature for at least 2 hours. Drain and dry thoroughly with paper towels.

Put cucumbers in casserole with butter, dill, chives, and onion. Bake for 25 minutes.

Remove from oven; add heavy cream. Stir over medium heat for about 5 minutes (do not allow to boil). Cream will thicken. Sprinkle with parsley and small amount of Parmesan cheese. Serve hot.

TOTAL GRAMS   24.7
GRAMS PER SERVING   6.2

Crazy Cabbage

8 servings

1 cabbage, trimmed
1 onion, chopped
¼ pound bacon
2 garlic cloves
2 tablespoons olive oil
¼ cup chopped parsley
1 egg
1 tablespoon grated Parmesan cheese
seasoned salt
1 cup Chicken Stock

Preheat oven to 375° F.

Boil cabbage in salted water for 15 minutes. Remove and run under cold water. Core cabbage, leaving outer leaves intact. Chop core and inner leaves. Sauté cabbage, onion, bacon, and garlic together in olive oil.

Mix parsley with egg and Parmesan cheese. Beat well.

Mix egg mixture into sautéed cabbage.

Oil a deep casserole. Place large outer cabbage leaves in casserole. Fill middle with sautéed mixture. Pour *Chicken Stock* over mixture. Cover and bake for 1 hour. Remove cover and bake for 30 more minutes. Serve.

TOTAL GRAMS 37.8
GRAMS PER SERVING 4.7

Ratatouille

12 ½-cup servings

4½ tablespoons olive oil
3 medium-size zucchini, unpeeled, quartered, cut into 1-inch lengths
½ medium-size eggplant, unpeeled, cut into 1½-inch cubes
salt and pepper to taste
2 medium-size onions, chopped
5 cloves garlic, finely minced
2 green peppers, chopped
1 8-ounce can tomato sauce
½ teaspoon thyme
1 teaspoon basil
¼ cup finely chopped parsley
lemon wedges

Preheat oven to 350° F.

Heat 2½ tablespoons olive oil in large skillet, add zucchini, eggplant, salt, and pepper. Cook, stirring occasionally, for about 10 minutes.

Heat remaining 2 tablespoons olive oil in another skillet. Add onions, garlic, and peppers, and cook until lightly browned. Add tomato sauce and simmer, stirring occasionally, for about 10 minutes.

Add zucchini and eggplant mixture, then thyme, basil, and parsley. Pour in casserole, cover, and bake for about 20 minutes, or until vegetables are tender.

Can also be served cold with lemon wedges.

TOTAL GRAMS 48.6
GRAMS PER SERVING 4.0

Basic Fried Green Tomatoes

Not always available, I treat green tomatoes like jewels when I have them. The following are easy-to-prepare-and-enjoy recipes.

1 green tomato, washed and sliced
1 tablespoon garlic oil
1 tablespoon sweet butter

Heat garlic oil and butter together in small nonstick skillet. Place tomatoes in skillet and fry over medium heat on both sides until brown.

TOTAL GRAMS 6.3

Variation 1: Sprinkle with sugar substitute while cooking.
Variation 2: Sprinkle with seasoned salt while cooking.
Variation 3: Dip tomatoes in egg and then in grated Parmesan cheese before frying.

TOTAL GRAMS 7.1

Variation 4: Spoon ½ teaspoon of white wine on each slice as it cooks.

TOTAL GRAMS 6.5

Variation 5: When finished frying place a slice of Gruyére cheese and crumbled bacon on top of each slice and broil until cheese begins to bubble.

TOTAL GRAMS 6.4

Variation 6: Top with warm goat cheese and serve on lettuce, garnished with ½ avocado for a delicious lunch salad.

TOTAL GRAMS 12.4

Porcini Mushrooms

4 servings

4 large porcini mushrooms
2 tablespoons butter
2 tablespoons garlic oil
2 tablespoons white wine
4 tablespoons mascarpone cheese
2 tablespoons Tamari soy sauce

Wash, dry, and cut off stems of mushrooms.

Heat butter and garlic oil in a large skillet. Add mushrooms and cook for 3 minutes over medium heat. Turn once. Add wine to the pan. Turn mushrooms again. Place 1 tablespoon of mascarpone cheese in center of each mushroom. Sprinkle with soy sauce. Cook 1 minute longer and serve hot.

TOTAL GRAMS 9.6
GRAMS PER SERVING 2.4

Spicy Cauliflower Bake

6 servings

½ onion, minced
4 cloves garlic, minced
2 tablespoons butter
2 cups cauliflower, chopped
2 eggs, beaten
1 cup grated Parmesan cheese
5 slices bacon, cooked crisp and crumbled

Preheat oven 350° F.

Heat butter in a skillet. Add onions and garlic and cook until onions turn golden. Add cauliflower and continue to cook 1 minute more. Remove to a bowl. Add eggs, Parmesan cheese, and crumbled bacon.

Spoon into a buttered baking dish. Bake for 1 hour, or until brown.

TOTAL GRAMS 24.4
GRAMS PER SERVING 4.1

Crispy White Radish

2 servings

1 medium daikon white radish
garlic oil
seasoned salt

Using the large holes on a four-sided grader, shred radish. Fill a 9-inch skillet ¼ full with garlic oil. Heat oil until very hot. Fry radish until golden brown. Remove from oil with slotted spoon and drain on brown paper. Sprinkle with seasoned salt.

Better than French fries!

TOTAL GRAMS 0.7
GRAMS PER SERVING 0.3

Cheesy Brussels Sprouts

4 servings

20 brussels sprouts
garlic oil
2 tablespoons grated Parmesan cheese

Slice brussels sprouts in half. Heat enough garlic oil to ¼ fill a skillet. Fry brussels sprouts until golden on both sides.

Remove with a slotted spoon and allow to drain on brown paper. Place in a bowl and toss with Parmesan cheese.

TOTAL GRAMS 13.3
GRAMS PER SERVING 3.3

Rutabaga Home Fries

6 servings

½ large rutabaga, quartered
2 medium-size onions, sliced thin
5 shiitake mushrooms, sliced thin

Boil rutabaga in water until fork-soft. Drain and return to pan. Heat 2 minutes more to dry rutabagas. Slice to size of half dollars.

Melt butter in a nonstick skillet. Add onions and sauté until transparent. Add mushrooms and continue sautéeing until soft. Add rutabagas and sauté until brown and crisp.

TOTAL GRAMS 40.4
GRAMS PER SERVING 6.7

Irene's Turnips

4 servings

4 medium-sized turnips
seasoned salt to taste
2 tablespoons sweet butter
3 slices no-nitrate bacon

Boil turnips in salted water until fork-soft. Drain well and, using a potato masher, mash turnips until smooth. Cook bacon in a nonstick skillet. Remove bacon and leave fat in pan. Spoon turnips into pan and sauté in bacon fat until turnips absorb fat. Remove to a bowl, crumble bacon on top and serve.

TOTAL GRAMS 30.5
GRAMS PER SERVING 7.6

Chic Asparagus

4 servings

1 pound asparagus
3 tablespoons extra-virgin olive oil
2 tablespoons white wine
2 ounces goat cheese
2 sun-dried tomatoes in olive oil, minced

Wash and trim asparagus, and place them in a glass baking dish. Mix olive oil and wine together and sprinkle over asparagus. Dot with goat cheese and sun-dried tomatoes. Microwave on low speed for 5 minutes or until desired softness.

TOTAL GRAMS 16.2
GRAMS PER SERVING 4.1

Green Bean Chokes

4 servings

1 pound green beans
1 6-ounce jar marinated artichoke hearts
2 ounces Parmesan cheese shavings

Wash green beans and cut off ends. Place in a glass baking dish. Top with marinade from artichokes. Quarter artichoke hearts and spread over string beans. Add Parmesan shavings. Place in a microwave oven and cook at low speed for 5 minutes.

TOTAL GRAMS   42.7
GRAMS PER SERVING   10.7

Sauces

Cream Sauce

24 tablespoons

¼ pound sweet butter
3 egg yolks
¼ cup water
¼ cup heavy cream
dash of nutmeg

Place butter in top of double boiler over hot (not boiling) water. Add egg yolks one at a time. Beat constantly with rotary or hand electric beater. Add water and heavy cream. Continue to beat until sauce thickens, about 7 to 10 minutes. Add nutmeg as garnish.

TOTAL GRAMS   4.1
GRAMS PER SERVING   TRACE

Frozen Horseradish Cream

19 tablespoons

1 cup heavy cream
2 tablespoons white horseradish
1 teaspoon seasoned salt
2 teaspoons Dijon mustard

Whip heavy cream until stiff.

Mix together horseradish, salt, and mustard. Carefully fold mixture into whipped cream. Freeze until firm.

TOTAL GRAMS   11.3
GRAMS PER TABLESPOON   0.6

Hollandaise Sauce

24 tablespoons

2 tablespoons tarragon vinegar
½ teaspoon seasoned salt
1 tablespoon cold water
4 egg yolks
2 sticks butter, at room temperature
1 teaspoon lemon juice
1 tablespoon heavy cream

Combine vinegar and salt in saucepan and cook rapidly to reduce to half. Remove from heat and add water. Place yolks in saucepan and beat with wire whisk until creamy. Place pan over double boiler and begin to add butter a little at a time. Beat with whisk as butter is melting. When sauce is thick, add lemon juice and heavy cream. Beat again. Keep warm until ready to serve.

TOTAL GRAMS   5.3
GRAMS PER TABLESPOON   0.2

Tartare Sauce

16 tablespoons

¾ cup mayonnaise
1 tablespoon tarragon vinegar
1 teaspoon finely chopped onion
1 teaspoon capers
1 teaspoon finely chopped pickles
1 teaspoon finely chopped olives
1 teaspoon finely chopped parsley

Combine all ingredients. Mix well.
    Store in covered jar in refrigerator. Will keep for several weeks.

TOTAL GRAMS   4.6
GRAMS PER TABLESPOON   0.3

Cocktail Sauce

16 tablespoons

1 8-ounce can tomato sauce
1 tablespoon horseradish
1 teaspoon Worcestershire sauce
1 teaspoon lemon juice

Mix all ingredients. Chill thoroughly.

TOTAL GRAMS   18.4
GRAMS PER TABLESPOON   1.2

Pasta Sauce

14 ½-cup servings

2 pork chops
5 tablespoons olive oil
6 8-ounce cans tomato sauce
3 8-ounce cans water
3 large cloves garlic, minced
1 teaspoon salt
1 pound sweet or hot Italian sausages
1 pound chuck, ground
1 teaspoon oregano
1 teaspoon thyme
2 packets sugar substitute

Place pork chops and 2 tablespoons olive oil in large heavy pot. Brown chops well. Add tomato sauce, water, garlic, and salt.

Bring to slow boil. Allow to simmer.

Place sausages in heavy skillet without any oil. Prick sausages with fork. Cook until well browned on all sides. Slice into one-half-inch pieces. Drain well and discard drippings. Add to pork chop mixture.

Form ground chuck into 1 large ball and place in skillet with 3 tablespoons olive oil. As chuck is browning, slowly break up into small pieces. (This is done to allow meat to retain its juices.) When meat is lightly browned, add to pork chop mixture.

Simmer for 3 hours, stirring occasionally.

Add oregano and thyme the last ½ hour. When mixture is finished cooking, add sugar substitute.

TOTAL GRAMS 82.8
GRAMS PER SERVING 5.9

Green Sauce for Pasta

26 tablespoons

5 cloves garlic, minced
2 tablespoons dried basil
¼ teaspoon thyme
¼ cup grated Parmesan cheese
4 tablespoons chopped walnuts
6 tablespoons olive oil
6 tablespoons butter
2 tablespoons chopped parsley

Place garlic, basil, thyme, Parmesan cheese, walnuts, and 2 teaspoons oil in blender. Blend until smooth. Add remaining oil, 2 tablespoons at a time, and blend. Serve on pasta topped with 1 tablespoon butter per serving.

TOTAL GRAMS 12.1
GRAMS PER TABLESPOON 0.6

Mustard Sauce

20 tablespoons

4 tablespoons Dijon mustard
1 cup sour cream
2 tablespoons chopped chives

Mix ingredients well. Refrigerate.

TOTAL GRAMS　14.9
GRAMS PER TABLESPOON　0.8

Hot Barbecue Sauce

20 tablespoons

2 tablespoons butter
1 medium onion, chopped
1 clove garlic, minced
¼ cup tomato sauce
2 tablespoons wine vinegar
¼–½ teaspoon Tabasco sauce
3 packets sugar substitute
1 teaspoon salt
1 teaspoon dry mustard
¼ cup water

Melt butter in saucepan. Sauté onion and garlic until golden. Add remaining ingredients and bring to boil. Store in covered jar and refrigerate.

TOTAL GRAMS　11.5
GRAMS PER TABLESPOON　0.6

Lemon Barbecue Sauce

12 tablespoons

1 small clove garlic
½ teaspoon salt
¼ cup oil
¼ cup lemon juice
2 tablespoons chopped onion
½ teaspoon thyme
1 packet sugar substitute

Mash garlic clove in bowl. Add salt. Dissolve in oil and add remaining ingredients. Chill to blend.

Excellent on grilled fish.

TOTAL GRAMS   6.7
GRAMS PER TABLESPOON   5.5

Cranberry Sauce

8 ½-cup servings

2½ cups fresh cranberries
1½ cups water
1 package diet lemon or orange gelatin
8 packets sugar substitute
2 tablespoons cranberry or orange liqueur
1 tablespoon No-Cal raspberry syrup
pinch salt

Cook cranberries in water over low heat until they pop open. Drain and press through sieve, and add boiling water until there are 1½ cups liquid.

Dissolve gelatin, sugar substitute, and flavorings in hot liquid.
Chill until firm. Slice to serve.

TOTAL GRAMS   67.2
GRAMS PER SERVING   9.7

Cheese Sauce

18 tablespoons

¾ cup heavy cream
⅓ cup water
¾ pound (1½ cups) Cheddar cheese, diced
1 teaspoon mustard
1 teaspoon salt
½ teaspoon paprika

In double boiler combine ingredients for cheese sauce. Simmer slowly. Stir constantly until smooth.

TOTAL GRAMS   12.5
GRAMS PER TABLESPOON   0.6

Parsley Butter Sauce

4 2-tablespoon servings

4 sprigs parsley, chopped (tops only)
1 small clove garlic, chopped fine
¼ pound sweet butter, melted
¼ teaspoon Worcestershire sauce

In a skillet add parsley and garlic to melted butter. Cook for 1 minute over medium heat. Add Worcestershire sauce.
    Serve immediately.
    (If you must reheat this sauce, use very low heat.)

TOTAL GRAMS   3.6
GRAMS PER SERVING   0.9

Joan's Ricotta Sauces

10 tablespoons

For Pork:
½ cup ricotta cheese
2 tablespoons olive oil
1 packet sugar substitute
1 teaspoon orange rind
¼ teaspoon nutmeg
⅛ teaspoon ground cloves
⅛ teaspoon cinnamon

Mix all ingredients together. Refrigerate for ½ hour. Serve

TOTAL GRAMS	7.0
GRAMS PER TABLESPOON	0.7

For Chicken:
½ cup ricotta cheese
½ teaspoon curry powder
¼ teaspoon tumeric
¼ teaspoon cumin
2 tablespoons sour cream

Mix ingredients together and refrigerate for ½ hour.

TOTAL GRAMS	4.2
GRAMS PER SERVING	0.4

For Fish:
½ cup ricotta cheese
2 tablespoons heavy cream
1 teaspoon tarragon
1 teaspoon grated lemon peel
1 packet sugar substitute

Mix all ingredients together and refrigerate for ½ hour.

TOTAL GRAMS	5.5
GRAMS PER SERVING	0.6

Tomato Paste

80 tablespoons

10 tomatoes, chopped
½ teaspoon salt

Place tomatoes in a sauce pan. Sprinkle with salt. Simmer for ½ hour uncovered. Strain, mashing pulp into strainer as you push liquid through. Cool. Keep in refrigerator to use when cooking.

TOTAL GRAMS 50.0
GRAMS PER TABLESPOON 0.6

Vinegar- and Sugar-Free Ketchup

40 tablespoons

2 cups Tomato Paste
½ cup lemon juice
½ cup water
½ teaspoon salt
1 teaspoon oregano
⅛ teaspoon cumin
⅛ teaspoon nutmeg
⅛ teaspoon pepper
½ teaspoon dry mustard
dash garlic powder

Place all ingredients in a blender or food processor and blend well. Refrigerate.

TOTAL GRAMS 30.0
GRAMS PER TABLESPOON 0.7

Desserts

Mac-Nut Candy

10 candies

2 tablespoons No-Cal chocolate syrup
2 packets sugar substitute
6 tablespoons unsweetened coconut
10 large macadamia nuts

Mix syrup and sweetener. Spoon over coconut and mix well. Allow flavors to blend for 2 minutes. Roll nuts in coconut mixture until well covered. Place on wax paper in freezer for 10 minutes before serving.
   To store: Wrap well in wax paper and place in freezer bag.

TOTAL GRAMS   41.9
GRAMS PER SERVING   4.2

Almond Balls

12 balls

¼ teaspoon almond extract
2 packets sugar substitute
1 tablespoon coconut
3 tablespoons almond butter*
1 tablespoon mascarpone cheese

Mix almond extract and 1 packet sugar substitute. Spoon over coconut and mix well. Mix almond butter, cheese, and 1 packet sugar substitute until fully blended.
   Roll into ¼-inch balls and place in freezer for 10 minutes.
   To store: Wrap well in waxed paper and store in freezer bag.

TOTAL GRAMS   17.6
GRAMS PER SERVING   1.5

*Available at health food stores.

Almond Ball Cookies

12 cookies

1 Almond Ball *recipe*
2 tablespoons coconut

Preheat oven to 325° F.
    Follow *Almond Ball* recipe and add coconut.
    Drop by teaspoonsful onto greased cookie sheet.
    Bake for 10 minutes or until golden brown. Be careful not to burn bottoms.

TOTAL GRAMS 23.0
GRAMS PER SERVING 1.9

Pistachio Popcorn Balls

6 balls

1¼ cups fresh popcorn
3 tablespoons roasted pistachio nut butter*
1 dozen cold pistachio nuts

Mix all ingredients and form into tablespoon-size balls. Serve.

TOTAL GRAMS 7.6
GRAMS PER SERVING 1.8

Basic Frosting

13 tablespoons

¼ cup sugar-free vanilla pudding
¼ cup mascarpone cheese
¼ cup ricotta cheese

---

*Available at health food stores.

1 teaspoon vanilla extract
3 packets sugar substitute

Prepare pudding using heavy cream as liquid.

Place mascarpone, pudding, ricotta, and extract in bowl and whisk together.

Chocolate or butterscotch frosting may be made by substituting appropriate pudding flavor.

Use frosting on one of our sponge cakes.

TOTAL GRAMS   14.9
GRAMS PER SERVING   1.1

Baked Cream Frosting

2 ½-cup servings

1 Basic Frosting *recipe*
1 tablespoon No-Cal Pancake Syrup

Preheat oven to 350° F.

Place *Basic Frosting* in 2 small ramikins. Bake for ½ hour or until set. Remove from oven and spoon pancake syrup on top. Serve immediately.

TOTAL GRAMS   14.9
GRAMS PER SERVING   7.4

Cannoli Custard Frosting

Fills 1 cake

Follow *Basic Frosting* recipe directions and place mixture in freezer until it becomes a custard. May be used as cake frosting, between two cake layers, or enjoyed as a custard.

TOTAL GRAMS   14.9
GRAMS PER SERVING   1.2

Ice Cream

Ice cream is a very important part of this diet. It has long been enjoyed as the special, delicious climax of afternoon picnics, informal lunches, and formal dinners. Dr. Atkins has been known to eat it watching football on a Sunday afternoon.

Because we all love it so much, I have perfected seven (one for each day of the week) no-fail ice cream recipes. Two of the recipes (*Vanilla and Coffee*) you may have from the beginning of the diet. *Coconut Macadamia*, *Butter Pecan*, and *Maple Walnut* may be added to the Ongoing Weight Loss. Premaintenance welcomes *Raspberry Rapture* and *Chocolate*. Maintenance offers *Chunky Chocolate Fudge Ice Cream* plus two frozen yogurts and two sorbets.

Preparing these creamy delights is easy. All you need are these recipes and an ice cream maker. This may sound expensive but it need not be. Hand-churned ice cream makers sell for as low as $25. Using them is easy. The preparation time is a little longer because the custard must be refrigerated for two hours before you can churn it. The electric machines start at about $70 and go up. Two that are under $90 are The Big Chill® and Gelato Modo 11®. Both make delicious ice cream from these recipes. The custard is churned in a container you prefreeze in your freezer. The entire process takes about ½ hour once the prepared custard is cooled at room temperature. You will rejoice at the way these ice cream makers make dessert (ice cream) while you eat dinner.

Basic Ice Cream Custard

6 ½-cup servings

2 cups heavy cream
4 egg yolks
½ vanilla bean, slit open and scraped
8 packets sugar substitute

Heat cream in a heavy sauce pan on a low heat. Whisk in one egg yolk at a time. Add vanilla bean scrapings and whisk until custard begins to thicken. Remove from heat and cool. Beat one packet of sugar substitute at a time into cooled custard. At this point the custard is ready to add recipe ingredients that make it ice cream (see recipes that follow). Do not overlook the value of refrigerating the custard as it is and using it as a delicious, rich dessert. Or you could whisk in a tablespoon of brandy or brandy flavoring and serve it over berries. An elegant dessert, indeed.

TOTAL GRAMS　24.2
GRAMS PER SERVING　4.0

Chocolate Ice Cream

8 ½-cup servings

1 recipe Basic Ice Cream Custard
½ cup unsweetened cocoa
2 packets sugar substitute
2 tablespoons No-Cal chocolate syrup
2 tablespoons Sugar-Free Jell-O Chocolate Instant Pudding powder
2 tablespoons Godiva Liqueur (optional)

Prepare *Basic* recipe. Whisk in cocoa. Beat until smooth. Remove from stove and whisk in sugar substitute, chocolate syrup, pudding powder, and Godiva Liqueur. Cool to room temperature. Place custard in ice cream maker. Churn according to manufacturer's directions.

TOTAL GRAMS　58.8
GRAMS PER SERVING　7.4

Chunky Chocolate Fudge Ice Cream

9 ½-cup servings

1 recipe Chocolate Ice Cream
½ recipe Chocolate Fudge

Prepare *Chocolate Ice Cream* and *Chocolate Fudge* recipes. Cut fudge into ¼-inch squares. Add to ice cream maker just before ice cream is ready.

TOTAL GRAMS   87.1
GRAMS PER SERVING   9.7

Raspberry Rapture Ice Cream

8 ½-cup servings

1 recipe Basic Ice Cream Custard
2 tablespoons No-Cal raspberry syrup
1 tablespoon Framboise (red raspberry liqueur)
1 cup whole raspberries
2 packets sugar substitute

Prepare *Basic Ice Cream Custard.* Allow to cool.

Heat syrup and Framboise to the boiling point (do not boil). Remove from heat. Place raspberries in a small bowl. Sprinkle with sugar substitute. Add syrup and Framboise. Allow flavors to blend (about 5 minutes).

Whisk raspberry mixture into cooling custard. Cool to room temperature. Place in ice cream maker and churn.

TOTAL GRAMS   39.4
GRAMS PER SERVING   4.9

Vanilla Ice Cream

6 ½-cup servings

1 recipe Basic Ice Cream Custard
1 tablespoon vanilla extract
2 tablespoons Sugar-Free Jell-O Vanilla Instant Pudding powder

Prepare *Basic Ice Cream Custard.* While cooling, whisk in vanilla extract and pudding powder. Cool to room temperature.

Place in ice cream maker and churn according to manufacturer's directions.

TOTAL GRAMS   30.2
GRAMS PER SERVING   5.0

Butter Pecan Ice Cream

8 ½-cup servings

1 recipe Basic Ice Cream Custard
2 tablespoons sweet butter
1 cup pecan halves
2 packets sugar substitute
1 tablespoon Sugar-Free Jell-O Butterscotch Instant Pudding powder

Prepare *Basic Ice Cream Custard.* Allow to cool.

Melt butter in a small skillet. Add nuts to pan. Sauté for one minute. Sprinkle with sugar substitute. Remove from heat and mix well, coating nuts completely. Whisk butterscotch pudding powder into cooling custard. Blend until smooth. Whisk nuts in. Cool to room temperature. Place in ice cream maker and churn according to manufacturer's directions.

TOTAL GRAMS   61.2
GRAMS PER SERVING   7.7

Coconut Macadamia Ice Cream

8 ½-cup servings

1 recipe Basic Ice Cream Custard
¼ cup unsweetened coconut
½ teaspoon rum extract
½ cup whole unsalted macadamia nuts
1 tablespoon Sugar-Free Jell-O Vanilla Instant Pudding powder
2 packets sugar substitute

Prepare *Basic Ice Cream Custard.* Allow to cool.

Place coconut on a small bowl and sprinkle rum extract on it. Stir to combine flavors. Whisk coconut, macadamia nuts, pudding powder, and sugar substitute into cooling custard. Cool to room temperature. Place in ice cream maker and churn according to manufacturer's directions.

TOTAL GRAMS 87.3
GRAMS PER SERVING 10.9

Maple Walnut Ice Cream

8 ½-cup servings

1 recipe Basic Ice Cream Custard
1 tablespoon maple extract
2 tablespoons sweet butter
2 packets sugar substitute
1 cup walnut halves

Prepare *Basic Ice Cream Custard.* Whisk in maple extract. Melt butter in a skillet. Add nuts and sauté for 1 minute. Sprinkle with sugar substitute and mix well. Add nuts to custard and cool to room temperature. Place in ice cream maker and churn according to manufacturer's directions.

TOTAL GRAMS 34.6
GRAMS PER SERVING 4.3

Decaf-Coffee Ice Cream

8 ½-cup servings

1 recipe Basic Ice Cream Custard
1 cup very strong decaffinated coffee
2 tablespoons sugar-free French vanilla creme coffee*

Prepare *Basic Ice Cream* recipe. Brew coffee by using 2 cups water and 4 tablespoons decaf. When brewed, simmer over a low flame until it reduces by half. Remove from heat. Whisk in vanilla creme coffee and allow to cool. Whisk coffee mixture into *Basic Ice Cream Custard.* Cool to room temperature. Place in ice cream maker and churn according to manufacturer's directions.

TOTAL GRAMS   28.1
GRAMS PER SERVING   3.5

Peach Melba Frozen Yogurt

8 ½-cup servings

2 cups Dannon Lite vanilla yogurt
2 egg yolks
8 packets sugar substitute
3 Stewed Peaches, *diced*
1 tablespoon No-Cal raspberry syrup

Whisk yogurt, egg yolks, and sugar substitute together over a low heat. Stir until mixture begins to thicken. Remove from heat. Add peaches and raspberry syrup. Mix well. Cool to room temperature. Place in ice cream maker and allow to churn according to manufacturer's directions.

TOTAL GRAMS   65.7
GRAMS PER SERVING   8.2

---

*Available in coffee department of supermarket.

Chocolate Yogurt

4 ½-cup servings

2 cups Dannon Lite vanilla yogurt
2 egg yolks
4 packets sugar substitute
2 tablespoons No-Cal chocolate syrup
2 tablespoons Godiva Liqueur (optional)

Heat yogurt on low heat. Whisk in egg yolks, sugar substitute, No-Cal syrup, and Godiva Liqueur. Stir until mixture begins to thicken. Remove from heat and cool to room temperature. Place in ice cream maker and churn according to manufacturer's directions.

TOTAL GRAMS   65.7
GRAMS PER SERVING   16.2

Raspberry Sorbet

8 ½-cup servings

1 cup heavy cream
2 egg yolks
1 teaspoon lemon extract
8 packets sugar substitute
1 cup raspberries
½ cup No-Cal raspberry syrup
¼ cup Framboise (red raspberry liqueur)

Heat cream on low heat. Whisk in egg yolks one at a time. Add lemon extract and 4 packets of sugar substitute. Whisk until mixture begins to thicken. Remove from heat.

Wash and dry raspberries. Place in a bowl. Sprinkle with 4 packets of sugar substitute. Add raspberry syrup and Framboise. Mix well.

Whisk raspberry mixture into yogurt. Cool to room temperature. Place mixture in ice cream maker and churn according to manufacturer's directions.

TOTAL GRAMS 37.4
GRAMS PER SERVING 4.7

Grapefruit Sorbet

8 ½-cup servings

1 cup heavy cream
2 egg yolks
8 packets sugar substitute
1 cup fresh grapefruit juice
1 package sugar-free lemon Jell-O
¼ cup Cointreau (fruit liqueur)

Heat heavy cream on low heat. Whisk in one egg yolk at a time. Remove from heat. Whisk in sugar substitute.

Heat grapefruit juice to boiling. Pour over Jell-O and mix until Jell-O completely disolves. Whisk in Cointreau. Mix grapefruit mixture with heavy cream. Blend very well. Place in ice cream maker and churn according to manufacturer's directions.

TOTAL GRAMS 46.6
GRAMS PER SERVING 5.8

Italian Rum Cake

12 servings

1 recipe Lemon Sponge Cake
1 recipe Cannoli Custard
1 tablespoon rum or rum extract
1 recipe Chocolate Frosting

Bake two layers of *Sponge Cake* and cool. Mix rum with *Custard*. Spread custard on top on one cake layer. Add second layer. Cover with *Frosting*.

TOTAL GRAMS 61.9
GRAMS PER SERVING 5.2

Confetti Mold

8 servings

1 package diet strawberry gelatin
1 package diet lime gelatin
1 package diet orange gelatin
3 packages diet lemon gelatin
1 cup heavy cream
1 teaspoon vanilla extract

Prepare first 3 diet gelatins separately, using 1½ cups water each. Refrigerate each in separate shallow pans until thoroughly firm. Dice each into tiny cubes.

Mix all 3 packages of lemon diet gelatin with 2 ¾ cups water. Allow to thicken. When mixture is very thick, but not firm, add heavy cream. Thicken again. Fold in all flavors of gelatin cubes and vanilla extract. Chill until thoroughly firm.

TOTAL GRAMS 23.0
GRAMS PER SERVING 2.9

Chocolate Peanut Butter Cookies

24 cookies

¾ cup soy flour
2 teaspoons cocoa
1½ teaspoons baking powder
4 packets sugar substitute
pinch salt
⅓ cup peanut butter
1 egg, beaten
1 teaspoon melted butter
½ cup heavy cream
1 teaspoon vanilla extract
½ teaspoon chocolate extract

Preheat oven to 400° F.

Sift dry ingredients into bowl.

Combine peanut butter with remaining ingredients and add to flour mixture. Stir until blended.

Drop by teaspoon onto greased cookie sheet. Bake for 10–12 minutes until brown.

TOTAL GRAMS   76.8
GRAMS PER COOKIE   3.2

Lemon Sponge Cake

8 servings

½ cup heavy cream
1 cup soy flour
1½ teaspoons baking powder
dash salt
3 eggs
8 packets sugar substitute
2 teaspoons vanilla
1 teaspoon lemon extract

Preheat oven to 300° F.

Scald cream and remove from heat.

Sift flour, baking powder, and salt together.

Beat eggs and sugar substitute thoroughly until thick and lemon colored. Blend in flour mixture just until smooth. Add warm cream and extracts to mixture. Pour batter immediately into a 9-inch greased tube pan. Bake for 30 minutes.

TOTAL GRAMS   32.2
GRAMS PER SERVING   4.5

Spice Cake

8 servings

½ cup heavy cream
1 cup soy flour
1½ teaspoons baking powder
pinch salt
½ teaspoon cinnamon
⅛ teaspoon ground cloves
¼ teaspoon nutmeg
3 eggs
8 packets sugar substitute
1 teaspoon brandy extract
2 teaspoons vanilla extract

Preheat oven to 325° F.

Scald cream and remove from heat. Sift flour, baking powder, salt, and spices together.

Beat eggs with sugar substitute until very thick. Blend in flour mixture until smooth. Add warm cream and extracts to mixture. Pour batter immediately into 8-inch greased layer pan. Bake for 30 minutes.

TOTAL GRAMS **34.5**
GRAMS PER SERVING **4.6**

Chocolate Sponge Layer Cake

8 servings

½ cup soy flour
½ teaspoon baking powder
pinch salt
1 tablespoon unsweetened cocoa
2 eggs
8 packets sugar substitute
1 teaspoon vanilla extract
1 teaspoon chocolate extract

Preheat oven to 325° F.

Sift flour, baking powder, salt, and cocoa together.

Beat eggs with sugar substitute until very thick.

Stir in extracts. Fold in flour mixture. Bake in 8-inch greased layer pan for 30 minutes. Makes 1 layer.

TOTAL GRAMS **19.2**
GRAMS PER SERVING **2.4**

Marzipan

24 1-inch forms

1 7-ounce package unsweetened coconut, finely grated
1 package diet gelatin (any fruit flavor)
1 cup ground almonds
½ cup heavy cream
4 packets sugar substitute
½ teaspoon vanilla extract
½ teaspoon almond extract

Combine all ingredients. Shape into any designs you like—fruits, vegetables, and so forth. (Food coloring may be added to simulate true details.)

Chill until forms hold their shape.

TOTAL GRAMS 84.0
GRAMS PER SERVING 3.5

Almond Pie Crust

1 pie crust

1 cup soy flour
½ cup ground almonds
2 packets sugar substitute
pinch cinnamon
⅓ cup butter, chilled

Preheat oven to 400° F.

Stir first 4 ingredients together. Cut in butter. Work well into dry ingredients.

Cover with wax paper and refrigerate for 1 hour.

Place in pie pan by tablespoons, patting sides and bottom with back of spoon. Use fork tines to decorate edges of pie crust and to prick holes in bottom and sides of crust. Place empty disposable pie plate over pie (to keep crust from puffing). Bake for 30 minutes until solid and brown around edges. Remove second pan, cover edges with foil, and allow center to brown thoroughly (about 5 minutes). Cool.

Substitute for *Pie Shell* when on Maintenance.

TOTAL GRAMS   36.0

Lemon Chiffon Pie

8 servings

3 egg yolks
1½ cups water
2 packets sugar substitute
1 package diet lemon gelatin
2 tablespoons lemon juice
1 teaspoon lemon extract
½ teaspoon grated lemon rind
3 egg whites
⅛ teaspoon salt
1 recipe Pie Shell, *baked*

Combine egg yolks, 1 cup water, and sugar substitute in a saucepan. Simmer, stirring constantly, until mixture begins to boil. Remove from heat, and stir in gelatin. Add remainder of water, lemon juice, lemon extract, and rind. Chill until somewhat thickened.

Beat egg whites and salt until mixture stands in stiff peaks. Stir gelatin mixture slightly, and fold in egg whites. Pour into prepared *Pie Shell*. Chill until firm.

TOTAL GRAMS   57.6
GRAMS PER SERVING   7.2

Coconut Cream Pie

10 servings

½ cup coconut
⅛ cup Cointreau
1 tablespoon butter
2½ cups heavy cream
1 envelope unflavored gelatin
¼ cup cold water
6 packets sugar substitute
4 egg whites at room temperature
2 teaspoons vanilla
1 recipe Pie Shell *(optional)*

Place coconut in flameproof bowl. Heat Cointreau and ignite. Pour over coconut. (Flames will be high.)

Heat butter in skillet. Add coconut and lightly toast it. Remove 2 tablespoons toasted coconut and set aside. Add 1 cup heavy cream to skillet. Simmer.

Sprinkle gelatin over cold water. Mix well. Add to cream. Simmer and stir until it begins to thicken. Remove from heat. Add 3 packets sugar substitute. Cool.

Beat egg whites until stiff with 1 packet of sugar substitute.

Fold egg whites into cool cream mixture.

Pour mixture into pie plate sprayed with imitation grease.

Refrigerate until firm.

Beat 1½ cups heavy cream with vanilla and 2 packets sugar substitute. Pile on top of firm cream mixture. Refrigerate for a least 2 hours before serving. Sprinkle with remaining coconut.

TOTAL GRAMS 34.5
GRAMS PER SERVING 3.5

Chocolate Mint Pie

8 servings

½ cup chopped pecans or walnuts
1 recipe Pie Shell
2 ounces unsweetened chocolate
2 tablespoons hot water
2 teaspoons peppermint extract
1 teaspoon vanilla
1 tablespoon creme de cacao
9 packets sugar substitute
2 cups heavy cream

Preheat oven to 275° F.

Sprinkle chopped nuts over *Pie Shell* and bake for 1 hour until lightly browned and crisp to touch. Cool, preferably leaving in oven until cool.

Melt chocolate in double boiler, stir in water, and cook until thickened. Remove from heat, and add peppermint extract, vanilla, crème de cacao, and sugar substitute.

Whip heavy cream with 1 packet of sugar substitute. Fold 1 cup whipped cream in chocolate mixture.

Spoon into meringue shell and chill for 2–3 hours.

Just before serving, spread remaining 1 cup whipped cream over top.

TOTAL GRAMS   45.0
GRAMS PER SERVING   5.6

Cheesecake

12 servings

16 ounces cream cheese at room temperature
3 eggs
1 cup crème fraîche or sour cream
½ vanilla bean, scraped
12 packets sugar substitute

Preheat oven 350° F.

Place all ingredients in a blender and blend for 15 minutes. Pour mixture into a 9 inch spring pan. Place in a pan of hot water in oven. If water evaporates during baking add more hot water to it. Bake for 1 hour, turn off oven and leave cake in oven 1 hour more.

TOTAL GRAMS 15.6
GRAMS PER SERVING 1.3

Coffee Cream Layer Cake

10 servings

5 eggs, separated, at room temperature
6 packets sugar substitute
2 cups heavy cream
1½ teaspoons instant decaffinated coffee
½ tablespoon gelatin
1 tablespoon cold water
3 tablespoons butter, at room temperature
2 teaspoons mocha extract
½ cup chopped walnuts

Preheat oven to 275° F.

Butter 3 round layer cake pans.

Beat egg whites until they form soft peaks. Add 1 packet sugar substitute and beat until stiff. Divide among 3 pans. Bake for 45 minutes.

Combine 1 cup heavy cream and instant decaf coffee in top of double boiler. Stir with wire whisk until powder dissolves. Dissolve gelatin in cold water. Add gelatin to coffee mixture and heat just to boiling. Stir constantly with whisk. Remove from heat. Beat in 4 egg yolks, 1 yolk at a time. Add butter and beat well until dissolved. Add extract and remaining sugar substitute. Put in freezer to cool.

Whip remaining cup heavy cream until stiff.

When coffee mixture is cool, fold into whipped cream and refrigerate until layers are cooked and cooled. Pile cream between layers of meringue as you would frost a layer cake. Top with cream, making sure to cover sides.

Sprinkle nuts on top and sides. Refrigerate until serving time.

TOTAL GRAMS 35.0
GRAMS PER SERVING 3.5

Lemon-Lime Mousse

8 servings

½ cup butter
9 egg yolks
juice of 2 lemons
juice of 2 limes
6 packets sugar substitute
2 teaspoons grated lemon rind
4 egg whites
1½ cups heavy cream
1 teaspoon vanilla extract

Melt butter in skillet.

Beat in egg yolks, one at a time, with wire whisk. Remove from heat. Add juice from lemons and limes, 4 packets sugar substitute, and lemon rind. Beat well. Cool.

Beat egg whites with 1 packet sugar substitute until stiff. Fold into lemon-lime mixture. Chill.

Whip heavy cream with 1 packet sugar substitute and vanilla extract. Fold into chilled mixture. Refrigerate for at least 2 hours.

TOTAL GRAMS   46.2
GRAMS PER SERVING   5.8

Pumpkin Chiffon

8 servings

1 envelope unflavored gelatin
½ teaspoon salt
½ teaspoon nutmeg
½ teaspoon cinnamon
¼ teaspoon ginger
½ cup cold water
2 egg yolks, slightly beaten
1 cup heavy cream
1¼ cups canned pumpkin

8 packets sugar substitute
2 egg whites

Combine gelatin, salt, and spices. Add ¼ cup water. Stir. Mix egg yolks with heavy cream, ¼ cup water, and pumpkin in top of double boiler. Add gelatin mixture. Cook over boiling water for 10 minutes, stirring constantly. Refrigerate until thick as unbeaten egg whites. Stir occasionally. Add sugar substitute (taste for sweetness).

Beat egg whites until stiff. Fold chilled pumpkin mixture into egg whites. Be careful not to break down volume of egg whites. Turn into 1½-quart soufflé dish. Refrigerate.

TOTAL GRAMS   30.2
GRAMS PER SERVING   3.8

The 'Pop' Pop

6 popsicles

1½ cups sugar-free fruit-flavored soda
6 teaspoons cream
sprinkle of sugar substitute (optional)

Mix all ingredients together.

Fill plastic molds for popsicles (1 mold holds 6 popsicles) with mixture. Insert stick if desired. (It is best to do this when popsicles are partially frozen.)

Freeze.

TOTAL GRAMS   2.6
GRAMS PER SERVING   0.4

Peanut Butter Cookies

40 cookies

½ cup chunk-style, sugar-free peanut butter
¾ cup heavy cream
½ cup chopped pecans
2 teaspoons vanilla
4 packets sugar substitute
2 tablespoons soy flour
1 teaspoon baking powder

Preheat oven to 375° F.
    Spray a cookie sheet with oil substitute.
    Mix all ingredients in bowl. Blend well.
    Drop on cookie sheet by teaspoonfuls. Bake for about 10 minutes.

TOTAL GRAMS 52.7
GRAMS PER COOKIE 1.3

Chocolate Fudge

15 squares

1 package Sugar-Free Jell-O Chocolate Instant Pudding
4 packets sugar substitute
½ cup heavy cream
1 tablespoon crème de cacao

3 heaping tablespoons chunk-style, sugar-free peanut butter
    Mix all ingredients together except peanut butter. Place over low flame and add peanut butter. Heat until peanut butter melts. Stir until well blended.
    Spray a small baking pan with oil substitute. Spoon mixture into pan. Refrigerate until firm. Slice into at least 15 squares.

TOTAL GRAMS 28.3
GRAMS PER SQUARE 1.9

Brownies

30 squares

½ cup butter, at room temperature
2 eggs
1 1-ounce square unsweetened chocolate
2 teaspoons chocolate extract
2 tablespoons water
2 tablespoons soy flour
½ cup coarsely chopped walnuts
8 packets sugar substitute
3 tablespoons crème de cacao

Preheat oven to 350° F.

Cream butter with electric hand mixer. Add eggs one at a time, beating well.

Melt chocolate with extract and water in top of double boiler. (If it gets too thick, add a little more water.)

Add melted chocolate, soy flour, chopped walnuts, and sugar substitute to butter. Mix well. Taste for sweetness. Add more sugar substitute if needed.

Grease a 1½-quart flat baking dish.

Pour in chocolate mixture. Bake 15 minutes. Do not overcook. Remove from oven. Sprinkle crème de cacao over top. Cool. Cut into at least 30 squares.

TOTAL GRAMS 59.9
GRAMS PER SQUARE 2.0

Pie Shell

1 pie shell

4 egg whites
pinch of salt
4 teaspoons crème de cacao

Preheat oven to 250° F.

Place egg whites and salt in bowl. Beat together until frothy. Gradually add crème de cacao. Continue beating until whites are stiff, glossy, and stand in stiff peaks.

Grease a pie plate. Pour meringue into pie plate and form crust with back of spoon.

Bake for 1 hour.

How to Beat Egg Whites for Meringues:
Eggs will beat better at room temperature, but separate better when cold. The trick is to separate them when cold, then let stand until they reach room temperature.

The best way to beat egg whites is with an electric hand beater; however, a rotary beater will also do the job.

TOTAL GRAMS   16.0

Stewed Peaches

10 peach halves

5 ripe summer peaches, peeled
3 tablespoons No-Cal raspberry syrup

Place peaches and syrup in a small pan. Simmer covered for 20 minutes.

Serve hot or refrigerate.

TOTAL GRAMS   48.9
GRAMS PER PEACH HALF   4.9

Beverages

Hot Chocolate

1 serving

⅓ cup cream
⅔ cup water
1 teaspoon unsweetened cocoa
1 packet sugar substitute
½ teaspoon vanilla

Place all ingredients in sauce pan. Heat to boiling point, but do not boil. Stir constantly.
   Serve in mug.

TOTAL GRAMS   5.1

Cappucino

1 serving

1 recipe Hot Chocolate
½ teaspoon instant coffee
½ teaspoon brandy extract
1 cinnamon stick

Make *Hot Chocolate.* Add coffee and brandy extract.
   Serve in mug with cinnamon stick.

TOTAL GRAMS   5.1

Spicy Cocktail

2 servings

2 cups Beef Stock
4 teaspoons tomato sauce
½ teaspoon onion juice or grated onion
½ teaspoon Worcestershire sauce
2 drops Tabasco sauce

Combine all ingredients Mix well. Serve hot or cold.

TOTAL GRAMS 22.2
GRAMS PER SERVING 11.1

Orange Cooler

4 servings

1 package sugar-free orange Jell-O
2 egg whites, beaten stiffly
2 teaspoon lemon rind, grated
1 teaspoon orange extract
2 packets sugar substitute
4 strawberries
4 ice cubes
4 lemon slices

Prepare gelatin according to package directions and cool.

Beat in stiff egg whites with wire whisk. Add lemon rind, orange extract, and sugar substitute.

Place in blender. Add strawberries and ice cubes. Blend at medium speed for 30 seconds.

Pour into glasses and garnish with lemon slices.

TOTAL GRAMS 10.2
GRAMS PER SERVING 2.5

Black and White Ice Cream Soda

1 serving

⅔ *glass diet chocolate soda*
1 tablespoon No-Cal chocolate syrup
2 tablespoons heavy cream
2 scoops Vanilla Ice Cream

Mix No-Cal syrup and heavy cream into soda. Add *Ice Cream.*

TOTAL GRAMS   5.2

Blender-Thick Raspberry Shake

2 servings

2 scoops Vanilla Ice Cream
3 tablespoons heavy cream
2 tablespoons No-Cal raspberry syrup
1 8-ounce bottle diet ginger ale

Place ingredients in blender. Blend for 1 minute at medium speed.

TOTAL GRAMS   7.9
GRAMS PER SERVING   4.0

Chocolate Shake

1 serving

1 envelope unflavored gelatin
1 cup diet chocolate soda
1 tablespoon unsweetened cocoa
4 ice cubes
⅓ cup heavy cream
1 packet sugar substitute
dash of salt

Place gelatin, ¼ cup soda, and cocoa in saucepan. Stir well.

Heat slowly to boiling point. Be sure gelatin dissolves completely. Cool.

Place ice cubes in blender. Add cooled gelatin mixture, heavy cream, ¾ cup soda, sugar substitute, and salt.

Blend at high speed for 30 seconds.

Serve in tall glass. It will become thicker as it sets. Stir vigorously.

TOTAL GRAMS   6.1

Shape-Up Shake

1 serving

1 envelope sugar-free lime Jell-O
1 cup diet lime soda
4 ice cubes
⅓ cup heavy cream
1 packet sugar substitute

Place gelatin and ¼ cup soda in saucepan. Heat to boiling point, stirring constantly. Be sure gelatin dissolves.

Cool.

Place ice cubes in blender, add gelatin mixture, heavy cream, ¾ cup soda, and sugar substitute.

Blend at high speed for 30 seconds.
Serve in tall glass. It will become thicker as it sets. Stir vigorously.

TOTAL GRAMS   3.0

Mocha Drink

1 serving

1 cup brewed decaffinated coffee
1 cup diet chocolate soda
1 tablespoon No-Cal chocolate syrup
4 ice cubes
¼ teaspoon cinnamon
2 tablespoons heavy cream
1 organic egg
1 packet sugar substitute (optional)

Place all ingredients in a blender and blend until smooth.

TOTAL GRAMS   2.3

Spiced Iced Decaf Coffee

4 servings

2 tablespoons decaffinated instant coffee
5 whole allspice
5 whole cloves
dash cinnamon
3 cups boiling water
8 ice cubes
4 teaspoons heavy cream

Combine all ingredients except cream in a 1-quart container. Cover and refrigerate 1 hour or more.

Strain. Pour over ice cubes into 4 tall glasses.

Add 1 teaspoon cream to each glass.

TOTAL GRAMS   1.2
GRAMS PER SERVING   0.3

Sweet Lemonade with Lecithin

4 servings

1 cup water
¼ cup lemon juice
2 packets sugar substitute
2 egg whites
1 teaspoon vanilla
½ teaspoon orange extract
dash salt
8 ice cubes
2 teaspoons lecithin

Place all ingredients except ice cubes and lecithin in a blender. Blend until thick.

Add 1 ice cube at a time and blend until frothy.

Remove from blender and stir in lecithin. Pour into 4 glasses. Stir again and serve immediately.

TOTAL GRAMS 21.7
GRAMS PER SERVING 5.4

Hot Mint Chocolate Nog

1 serving

1 cup Pelican Punch herbal tea*
2 teaspoons No-Cal chocolate syrup
1 teaspoon chocolate extract
1 packet sugar substitute
1 organic egg
2 tablespoons heavy cream

Place all ingredients in blender. Blend well.

TOTAL GRAMS 1.4

---

*Available in specialty and health food stores.

Appendices

Special Menus for Entertaining

FORMAL DINNER

Serves 12

HORS D'OEUVRES

Fran's Special Pâté
Deviled Salmon Eggs
Caribbean Crabmeat

APPETIZER

Honeydew and Seafood

SOUP

Cold Avocado Soup

SALAD

Tricolor Salad with 3 Cheeses

ENTRÉE

Stuffed Steak
or
Stuffed Flounder

VEGETABLES

Spicy Cauliflower Bake
Cheesy Brussels Sprouts

TO CLEAR THE PALLET

Small scoop of Grapefruit Sorbet

DESSERT

Spice Cake with Coconut Macadamia Ice Cream

BEVERAGES

Cappucino
tea
decaffinated coffee with cream and sugar substitute

BARBECUE

Serves 12

WHEN FOLKS ARRIVE

Guacamole with cucumber slices
Sour Cream Clam Dip with pork rinds
cheese tray

ON THE COALS

Dr. Atkins' Fromage Burgers
Luscious Lamb
Broiled Tarragon Lobster Tails (cook on coals instead of broiling)
chicken marinated in Hot Barbecue Sauce

THE SALADS

Cole Slaw
Mock Potato Salad

SWEETS

Confetti Mold
Coffee Ice Cream
Almond Ball Cookies
Chocolate Sponge Layer Cake

DRINKS

Spicy Cocktail
Sweet Lemonade with Lecithin
Orange Cooler

BUFFET DINNER

Serves 20

APPETIZING TABLE

Fresh Spring Salmon Mousse
Spicy Spare Ribs
Chinese Fish Balls
Heavenly Wings
Salad Niçoise with Fresh Tuna
assorted olives

ENTRÉE TABLE

Kayzie's Rabbit
Moussaka
Shrimp and Scallops Marc
Coq Au Vin with Shiitake Mushrooms

DESSERT TABLE

Lemon-Lime Mousse
Chocolate Mint Pie
Cheesecake
Raspberry Rapture Ice Cream

CANDY TRAY

Almond Balls
Chocolate Fudge
Pistachio Popcorn Balls

BEVERAGES

Cappucino
tea
decaffinated coffee
with cream and sugar substitute

DESSERT BUFFET ATKINS STYLE

Serves 12

2 CAKES

> Italian Rum Cake
> Coffee Cream Layer Cake

2 PIES

> Coconut Cream Pie
> Lemon Chiffon Pie

3 KINDS OF COOKIES

> Chocolate Peanut Butter Cookies
> Pistachio Popcorn Balls
> Brownies

2 FLAVORS OF ICE CREAM

> Butter Pecan Ice Cream
> Chocolate Ice Cream

BEVERAGES

> Spiced Iced Tea
> Cappuccino
> Hot Chocolate

Nutritional Supplementation

Twenty years ago I was almost a voice crying in the wilderness when I said you'd live a longer and healthier life if you ate a healthy diet *and* consumed vitamin and mineral supplements than you would if you ate a healthy diet alone. I have stubbornly persisted because the experiences of my forty thousand patients have affirmed and reaffirmed the correctness of that view. Now the virtues of supplements are becoming commonplace, supported by an increasing number of highly orthodox medical scientists and loudly proclaimed from the covers of major newsmagazines. In the end my viewpoint may become the conventional one, which would be a change of pace.

For all of you who are doing the Atkins diet I must insist on the importance of your supplements. During the two-week Induction phase of the diet, you will need supplements to maintain a proper nutritional balance. After that, you should go right on taking them because they're good for you.

Below is my Dieter's Formula. Find a multivitamin that gives you something close to this formula, and then take three capsules a day. People who weigh 200 pounds or more are to use the second, larger doses, provided in parentheses, of certain vitamins.

Dieter's Formula

Vitamin A	200 IU
Beta-Carotene	500 IU
Vitamin D-2	15 IU
Thiamine (HCl) (B$_1$)	5 mg
Riboflavin (B$_2$)	4 mg
Vitamin C (Calcium Ascorbate)	120 mg (150 mg)
Niacin (B$_3$)	2 mg
Niacinamide	5 mg
Pantethine (80%)	25 mg (30 mg)
Calcium Pantothenate (B$_5$)	25 mg
Pyridoxal-5-Phosphate	2 mg
Pyridoxine (HCl) (B$_6$)	20 mg
Folic Acid	100 mcg
Biotin	75 mcg
Cyanocobalamin (B$_{12}$)	30 mcg
Vitamin E (D alpha tocopherol)	20 IU
Copper (Sulfate)	200 mcg
Magnesium (Oxide)	8 mg
Chlorine (Bitartrate)	100 mg
Inositol	80 mg
PABA	100 mg
Manganese (Chelate)	4 mg
Zinc (Chelate)	10 mg
Citrus Bioflavonoids	150 mg
Chromium (Picolinate)	50 mcg
Molybdenum (Sodium)	10 mcg
Vanadyl Sulfate	15 mcg
Selenium	40 mcg
Octacosanol	150 mcg
N-Acetyl-1-cysteine	20 mg
L-Glutathione (reduced)	5 mg

The recommended formula comes in a base of lactobacillus, bulgaris and bifidus acidophilus, B-Complex and growth factors.

In addition to this formula, the next most important nutritional group for long-range supplementation are the essential fatty acids. You won't find these in a multivitamin formula because they exist physically as oils and don't mix with a dry powder capsule. There are two types of essential fatty acids that most of us need. One type is the omega-3 series that provides you with alpha linolenic acid (ALA). The other type is the omega-6 series called gamma linolenic acid (GLA).

To supplement with these important nutrients, take an essential oils formula containing approximately the following:

Flaxseed oil	400 mg
Borage oil	400 mg
Super EPA	400 mg

Carbohydrate Gram Counter

Foods	*Grams of Carbohydrate*
BEANS (COOKED)	
Black-eyed peas (1 cup)	34.0
Lima (½ cup)	25.0
Navy (1 cup)	40.0
Peanuts (2 oz.)	7.0
Red kidney (½ cup)	21.0
Soybeans (½ cup)	11.0
Split peas (1 cup)	52.0
Tofu (3½ oz.)	3.0
CONDIMENTS	
Anchovies (1 oz.)	0.1
Cocoa (1 tbs. unsweetened)	2.6
Horseradish (1 tsp.)	0.5
Mayonnaise (1 tbp)	0.3
Mustard:	
Dijon (1 tsp.)	0.3
regular (1 tsp.)	0.3
Pickles (1 medium dill)	1.4
Soy sauce (1 tbs)	1.7
Syrup:	
No-Cal chocolate	0.0
No-Cal strawberry	0.0
Vinegar:	
balsamic (1 tbs)	0.9
cider (1 tbs)	0.9
tarragon (1 tbs)	0.9
wine (1 tbs)	0.9
Worchestershire sauce (1 tbs.)	1.7

Foods	Grams of Carbohydrate
FATS/OILS	
Canola	0.0–trace
Olive	0.0–trace
Peanut	0.0–trace
Safflower	0.0–trace
Walnut	0.0–trace
FRUIT	
Apple, medium (2¾ in.)	18.0
Applesauce, unsweetened (½ cup)	13.0
Apricots (3 fresh)	14.0
Avocado:	
California	12.0
Florida	27.0
Banana (1)	26.0
Blackberries (1 cup)	19.0
Blueberries (1 cup)	21.0
Cantaloupe (½ 5-in. melon)	14.0
Cherries (½ cup)	13.0
Cranberries (1 cup)	11.0
Grapefruit (½, pink)	13.0
Grapefruit juice (1 oz.)	3.0
Grapes (1 cup)	15.0
Honeydew (½ 5-in.)	16.0
Kiwi (1 medium)	11.0
Lemon	6.1
Lemon juice (1 cup)	19.5
Lemon peel (1 tsp.)	0.5
Lime juice (1 oz.)	2.8
Mango (½ medium)	17.0
Olives:	
black (10 olives)	0.8
green, pitted	2.5

Foods	*Grams of Carbohydrate*
FRUIT	
Orange (1 medium)	18.0
Orange rind (1 tsp.)	0.5
Papaya (⅓ medium)	10.0
Peach (2½ in.)	10.0
Pear (3½ in.)	25.0
Pineapple (1 cup)	19.0
Plum (1 medium)	9.0
Prunes, cooked (½ cup)	39.0
Raspberries (1 cup)	17.0
Rhubarb (4 oz.)	4.2
Stewed peaches (1 cup)	20.0
Strawberries (1 cup)	13.0
GELATIN	
Gelatin	0.0
Sugar-Free Jell-O (all flavors)	0.0
GRAINS	
Bagel (1)	30.0
Bread:	
pumpernickel (1 slice)	13.0
whole-wheat (1 slice)	14.0
Corn muffin	20.0
Cornmeal (1 cup, cooked)	26.0
Farina (1 cup)	22.0
Noodles (1 cup)	37.0
Oatmeal (1 cup)	23.0
Pancake (1 buckwheat)	6.0
Popcorn (popped, 1 cup)	5.0
Rice:	
cooked (1 cup)	50.0
puffed (1 cup)	13.0
Soy flour (1 cup)	21.3
Waffle	28.0

Foods	*Grams of Carbohydrate*
HERBS	
Allspice (1 tbs.)	2.0
Basil (1 tsp.)	1.0
Caraway (1 tsp.)	1.0
Celery (1 tsp.)	1.0
Cinnamon (1 tsp.)	2.0
Coriander leaf (1 tsp.)	0.5
Dill seed (1 tsp.)	1.0
Garlic clove (1)	1.0
Ginger root:	
fresh (1 oz.)	3.0
ground (1 tsp.)	2.0
Saffron (1 tsp.)	1.0
Tarragon (1 tsp.)	0.5
Thyme (1 tsp.)	1.0
Vanilla, double strength (1 tsp.)	3.0
MILK PRODUCTS	
Butter (½ cup)	1.0
Cheese:	
American (1 oz.)	1.0
Boursin (1 oz.)	1.0
Camembert (1 oz.)	1.0
Cheddar (1 oz.)	1.0
cottage, creamed (1 cup)	7.0
cottage, uncreamed (1 cup)	5.0
cream (1 oz.)	2.0
feta (1 oz.)	1.0
fontina (1 oz.)	1.0
goat (1 oz.)	1.0
Jarlsberg (1 oz.)	1.0
marscarpone (1 oz.)	1.0
mozzarella (1 oz.)	1.0
muenster (1 oz.)	1.0
Parmesan (1 oz.)	1.0
provolone (1 oz.)	1.0
ricotta (1 oz.)	1.0

Foods	*Grams of Carbohydrate*
MILK PRODUCTS	
Roquefort (1 oz.)	1.0
Swiss (1 oz.)	1.0
Cream:	
heavy (1 oz.)	2.0
light (1 oz.)	2.0
sour (1 oz.)	2.0
whipped (1 oz.)	2.0
Half-and-half (1 oz.)	2.0
Milk (whole, 1 cup)	12.0
Yogurt, plain:	
lite (1 cup)	10.0
skim (1 cup)	13.0
whole (1 cup)	12.0
NUTS AND SEEDS	
Almond paste (1 oz.)	15.0
Almonds:	
1 oz.	6.0
12–15 nuts	3.0
Brazil (4 nuts)	3.0
Cashews (11–12, roasted)	5.0
Coconut (4 tbs.)	2.0
Grated coconut, unsweetened, (1 oz.)	6.5
Hazelnuts (filberts, 10 or 12)	3.0
Macadamia nuts (6)	2.0
Mixed (8–12 nuts)	3.0
Peanut butter:	
regular (1 oz.)	6.0
sugar-free (1 oz.)	3.0
Peanuts (4 tbs.)	7.0
Pecans (10 halves)	2.0
Pine nuts (Pignoli, 1 oz.)	3.3
Pistachio (30 nuts)	3.0
Pumpkin seeds (1 oz.)	4.0
Sesame seeds (1 oz.)	3.0
Soynuts (1 oz.)	7.0

Foods	Grams of Carbohydrate

NUTS AND SEEDS

Sunflower seeds (1 oz.)	6.0
Walnuts (8–10 halves)	3.0
Water chestnuts (1 oz.)	4.1

PROTEIN (LEAN, WITHOUT SKIN OR BREADING)

Eggs	0.0–trace
Fish	0.0–trace
Meat	0.0–trace
Poultry	0.0–trace

SOUPS

Chicken Consummè (1 cup)	2.0
Chicken Gumbo (1 cup)	9.0
Clam Stock (1 oz.)	0.6
Cream of Chicken (1 cup)	8.0
Cream of Mushroom (1 cup)	10.0
Turkey Rice (1 cup)	10.0

VEGETABLES

Asparagus (6 spears)	3.0
Bamboo shoots (1 cup)	7.8
Bean sprouts (1 cup)	6.5
Beans:	
green, boiled (½ cup)	3.3
yellow or wax (½ cup boiled)	3.7
Broccoli (1 stalk)	8.0
Brussels sprouts (4, or ½ cup)	5.0
Cabbage (½ cup)	4.0
Carrot (7 in.)	6.0
Cauliflower (1 cup)	5.0
Celery (3 pieces, 5 in.)	4.0
Chinese Cabbage (1 cup)	2.3
Cole slaw (4 oz.)	16.0

Foods	*Grams of Carbohydrate*
VEGETABLES	
Collards (1 cup)	9.0
Corn (1 ear, 5 in.)	16.0
Cucumber (6 slices, ⅛ in.)	2.0
Dandelion (½ cup)	6.0
Eggplant (diced, 1 cup)	8.2
Endive (½ cup)	2.0
Kale (½ cup)	2.0
Kohlrabi (⅔ cup)	7.0
Lettuce:	
Boston (1 head, 4 in.)	6.0
iceberg (⅙ head)	2.0
Romaine (2 leaves)	2.0
Mushrooms:	
regular (10 small or 4 large)	4.0
porchini (1 cup)	4.0
shiitake (1 cup)	4.0
Mustard greens (½ cup)	3.0
Okra (8)	5.0
Onion (2½ in.)	10.0
Parsley (1 tbs.)	1.0
Parsnips (1 tbs.)	18.0
Peas, (cooked, 1 cup)	19.0
Peppers:	
green (2 rings)	1.0
red (dried, 1 oz.)	5.0
Potato, baked (4¾ x 2⅓ in.)	21.0
Potato salad (½ cup)	16.0
Pumpkin:	
fresh (3½ oz.)	7.0
canned (1 cup)	19.0
Radish (4 medium)	1.0
Rutabagas (1 cup)	13.9
Scallions (1 tbs)	0.5
Spinach (½ cup)	4.0

Foods	Grams of Carbohydrate

VEGETABLES

Squash:

summer (1 small)	7.0
winter (1 small)	16.0
String beans (1 cup)	7.0
Sweet potato (5 in. x 2 in.)	36.0

Tomato:

cooked (½ cup)	5.0
juice (½ cup)	5.0
paste (1 oz.)	5.3
raw (2½ in.)	9.0
sauce (1 oz.)	5.3
sun-dried (average)	5.0
V-8 Juice (5.5-oz. can)	7.0

Turnips:

cooked (1 cup)	8.0
greens (1 cup)	5.0

SAMPLES OF CARBOHYDRATE-RICH "FATTENING" ITEMS

Apple pie (1 slice, homemade)	61.0
Apple turnover	30.0
Banana split	91.0
Blueberry Muffin (1 average)	17.0
Brownie (1 average homemade)	15.0
Burrito, bean	48.0
Cheeseburger (¼ pounder)	33.0
Corn bread stuffing (¼ cup)	69.0
Devil Dog	30.0
Donut (1 glazed)	22.0
Egg roll (1)	30.0
French toast (2 slices)	34.0
Hot dog with bun (1)	24.0
Ice cream soda (1 cup)	49.0
Jam (1 tbs. grape)	15.0
Macaroni and cheese (1 cup)	40.0

Foods	**Grams of Carbohydrate**
"FATTENING" ITEMS	
Onion rings (fast food order)	33.0
Pancake (1 buttermilk, plain)	15.0
Pecan pie (1 piece, homemade)	41.0
Pizza (1 slice)	24.0
Pop-Tart (frosted, blueberry)	34.0
Popsicle	17.0
Roast beef sandwich	20.0
Shake (medium)	90.0
Sherbert (½ cup lemon)	45.0
Taco, beef	14.0
Tapioca, cream (½ cup)	22.0
Vanilla shake (1 average)	50.0
Waffles (1 homemade, plain)	28.0
Whaler	64.0

Index